AN AVERAGE PILOT?

AN AVERAGE PILOT?

by

Christopher Masterman

Dales Large Print Books
Long Preston, North Yorkshire,
BD23 4ND, England.

British Library Cataloguing in Publication Data.

Masterman, Christopher
        An average pilot?

A catalogue record of this book is
available from the British Library

ISBN   978-1-84262-831-7 pbk

First published in Great Britain in 2010 by The Book Guild Ltd.

Cover illustration by arrangement with Book Guild

The right of Christopher Masterman to be identified as the
author of this work has been asserted by him in accordance with
the Copyright, Designs and Patents Act, 1988

Published in Large Print 2011 by arrangement with
Book Guild Publishing

Dales Large Print is an imprint of Library Magna Books Ltd.

Printed and bound in Great Britain by
T.J. (International) Ltd., Cornwall, PL28 8RW

Contents

1

Hawker Hart

Spring 2000.
'Hawker Hart,' he said suddenly.

Cedric and I were sitting in the sun-drenched conservatory of Glenside Manor. As usual with my twice weekly visits, we had run out of things to say after about twenty minutes and, because the short walk to the pub was no longer an option for him now that he found the road too steep, my thoughts had been turning towards saying my good-byes. Extricating myself from the nursing home was always the most difficult part of my visits; I never did master how to tell him that he had to remain while I went.

His memory span was by now non-existent so, a moment after I told him that he had to stay because he was being looked after in a hospital, he would ask again why he couldn't come with me and then again, and again, and again until I had made the front door, entered the combination, shaken

11

his hand and told him I would be back soon. Sometimes I couldn't separate myself from him at the door, so I would take him to his room, put him by his window from where he could see the outside of the front door, and tell him that I was just going to the toilet. I would then exit the front door into his sight. I would shout my good-byes; he would smile and wave me off, and I would make my escape.

I shook off my thoughts of departure and listened. I heard a faint aircraft drone from above, the sound perhaps of an aircraft with two piston engines.

'What?' I replied.

'Up there somewhere,' he said, pointing vaguely to his front and upwards, 'Two of them.'

Now this was really not credible. The Hart was perhaps the most famous member of a long line of similar two-seat military biplanes built by the British Hawker Aircraft Company in the 1930s, and in its way, the progenitor of the famous Hawker Hurricane – although its maximum speed of about 175 mph was not much more than half that of the Hurricane.

Two of them, though, flying over Wiltshire in 2000?

However, even at eighty-six years of age there was little wrong with Cedric's eyes or ears. So I scanned the sky and listened. Then, against one of the few clouds, I made out the silhouettes of two biplanes – both with the elegant pointed noses of the Hart stable. The sound of the engines did seem familiar – something like a pair of toned-down Hurricanes or Spitfires with their twelve cylinder, 'V' configuration, Rolls-Royce Merlin engines. Most Harts were fitted with Rolls-Royce Kestrel engines of 640 horsepower which, while not directly related to the Merlin, had a similar V12 cylinder configuration, and it seemed to me that a family resemblance was clearly audible.

I read in a local newspaper later that week that the two aircraft were indeed Hawker Hart derivatives that had been on their way to an air show on the South Coast of England.

Cedric had recognised the sound of Hawker Harts, a sound that he surely could not have heard since before World War Two. Yet, if I had then questioned him, he wouldn't have remembered that he had ever been married, although he still knew that he had one son – me – or where he had ever lived, what cars he had ever owned, who my wife was, who his grandchildren were, or where his room was in the Glenside Manor nursing home.

That, for me, was the most frustrating part of caring for a person with Alzheimer's disease. The sheer illogicality of it all; how could he be able to remember the sixty-year-old sound of an aircraft engine but not recognise my mother when shown her photo?

I looked at him smiling gently in the sunlight. Eighty-six years of age but looking ten years younger: eyes bright with the familiar drooped eyelids of a fighter pilot – drooped by continual scanning into the sun, good teeth, strong and beautiful hands, smartly dressed, his daily newspaper unopened on his knees – just as it would stay all day and every day. He was able to walk slowly around the grounds of the home, unaided when persuaded and cajoled, and capable of conducting a fluent but vacuous conversation. I was edging towards my sixtieth year and already my face was beginning to crumple into a facsimile of his. Would this be my fate too? I had led a far less interesting or useful life than he. He should have been able to reminisce on memories that I would never be able to match, but most of his life of more than one minute earlier was inaccessible to him – lost, but far from wasted.

He had first come to live with me and Ruth, who was then my wife, six years earlier. I had moved some of his possessions to our house and put others in storage. I had found his flying log books and had read through them casually. I knew of course, from stories he told in my childhood, that he had a passion for flying which he had single-mindedly pursued during his career in the British Royal Air Force (RAF). The log book entries at the start of his military flying career, however, give little indication of what was to come.

After leaving school, Cedric had spent two years working as an office boy in a foreign-exchange brokering firm in London, before becoming bored and successfully seeking a short-service commission with the RAF.

Twenty years old in 1935, he took his first flight as a student pilot on 10 May at No. 2 Flying Training School (FTS), RAF Digby in Lincolnshire, in an Avro Tutor biplane, two-seat elementary trainer powered by an Armstrong Siddeley Lynx radial piston engine of 240 horsepower; his instructor was a Sergeant Middleton. Eleven days and seven hours of instruction later, and after having been checked out by another instructor, Flying Officer Harman, he made his first solo flight. On 13 June he passed his first formal flying test with his flight commander, Flight Lieutenant Roberts. Finally, on 5 November 1935, with 96 hours of instruction completed which included aerobatics and instrument flying, he was deemed sufficiently schooled by the Tutor elementary trainer and Sergeant Middleton to be taken for his first flight by Flying Officer Hue-Williams in the next step up – a Hawker Hart.

He was sent solo on 3 December in a Hart after a further twelve hours of instruction, and on 14 January 1936 he was sent aloft in a single-seat Hawker Fury. This would have been a very exciting moment for Cedric because the Fury, although clearly related to the Hart, was a proper fighter with a maximum speed of just over of 200 mph and had been one of the RAF's front-line aircraft when first delivered in 1931 – but by 1936 it was already hopelessly outclassed and relegated to training duties.

More Hart and Fury flights followed until, on 28 February 1936 with 140 hours of flying completed, Cedric was awarded his RAF 'Wings'. His log book was endorsed by the Chief Flying Instructor of No 2 FTS to record him as having 'Average proficiency with no special faults'.

And so it began.

And so it was ending as we sat and listened in the grounds of Glenside Manor to the fading drone of the engines of the two Harts.

It is usually a long, incipient descent into the hell of Alzheimer's and, like other neural diseases such as multiple sclerosis, it is hard for an observer to recognise the onset, particularly if that observer is a close relative in a state of conscious or sub-conscious denial. Hindsight helps. Once it had been confirmed that Cedric was suffering from irreversible dementia, shortly after he came to live with Ruth and me, it was easy to look back and recall clear signs of mental problems over a number of years. At first these incidents are treated lightly, regarded as one-offs, a 'senior moment'; but the incidents become repetitive, more serious, embarrassing and dangerous – and the awful truth begins to dawn.

Ruth and I had emigrated to Canada from England in 1982. My father had retired from working in the City of London and he and my mother were living quietly in a small bungalow in Lincolnshire. Financially secure, their main concern was my mother's poor health – she was to die after another six years. Cedric was hale and hearty, a well-known and popular figure in the Lincolnshire market town of Sleaford. In 1985 he flew out from England to spend three weeks with us in our village to the west of Montreal. I hadn't spent so long with him since leaving home at the age of eighteen. The visit went well but we did comment to each other that he seemed rather selfish and not really interested in his two granddaughters. However, we enjoyed his visit and so did he.

The next year he invited himself out again. As before, I drove to collect him from Mirabelle international airport to the north of Montreal, about an hour's journey from my home. The traffic was bad and I was a little late getting to the arrivals hall. The plane had been early and already landed for some thirty minutes by the time I arrived. Most passengers appeared to have already cleared customs and collected their baggage, but Cedric was nowhere in sight. I went upstairs in the terminal to find the tourist information kiosk; I guessed that he would have made his way there on missing me. He was there, talking earnestly to a rather confused looking lady in the kiosk. He turned, saw and recognised me. 'Good Lord, Christopher, what are you doing here?' he exclaimed.

'Hello Cedric, I've come to collect you,' I replied. 'I'm sorry that I'm late, what are you doing?'

'This lovely lady and I are just arranging my hotel in Montreal, and a taxi to get me there.'

A look of relief came over the face of the lovely lady as I thanked her and took Cedric to my car for the drive home.

There were other incidents during his visit that summer that should have raised warning flags for me, but didn't. One day I lent him a car – his driving skills were still excellent – and sent him off to visit Upper Canada Village while I went to work. This village was an interesting recreation of early Canadian rural life, using buildings salvaged from the pathway of the St Lawrence Seaway and populated by actors posing as early settlers. It was about one-and-a-half hours' drive from the house. He set off at about 9 a.m. Ruth didn't go to work that day and was very surprised to find Cedric returned by lunchtime. 'Yes,' he explained, he had been to Upper Canada Village. 'But I didn't know I was supposed to go in.'

I left Cedric at the nursing home and returned to my house in the New Forest, thinking about Hawker Harts as I drove the twenty-minute journey. I gathered together his flying log books and personal papers. I started to study them in detail – if he couldn't remember what he had done in his life then I would have to become the guardian of his memories to pass on to my children and grandchildren.

2

Hawker Audax

I looked through Cedric's flying log books again and began to realise how complex his flying life had been, how very many different aircraft types he had flown – some, it seemed, with no prior training experience at all. Then there were the various WW2 combat theatres in which he had served: England, Scotland, Norway, Malta, Egypt, India and Burma. His Order of the British Empire (OBE), how had that come about? – not purely through piloting, surely. I found other wartime papers of his: maps, letters, newspaper cuttings and some memoirs written by him. I wanted to reconcile the log books with these other documents.

As I read through the log books I recognised the names of people he had flown with, people he had spoken about in later years, some of whom I had even met while growing up but who had meant nothing to me: Shrub Sellick, Gordon Burnside, Richard Rhys (who became our family solicitor), and Laurie Stickley. These memories then conjured up other names not in the log books but of RAF colleagues whom I had met while accompanying him at Farnborough air shows or Twickenham rugby matches: his great friend, and wedding best man, Freddie Rosier, Harry Broadhurst, Brian Eaton of the Royal Australian Air Force and Battle of Britain pilots – Johnny Johnson, Douglas Bader, Al Deere, Christopher Foxley-Norris and others. I realised that I knew a lot about his RAF life, but had not previously paid it the respect or attention it deserved.

I transcribed his log books onto a spreadsheet and cross-referred them with his other papers along with facts and anecdotes about him that I already knew. His name does not figure in many books describing famous exploits of RAF pilots and squadrons, neither did he achieve very high rank, but in many ways his career was very interesting and at times extraordinary.

Between May 1935 and May 1955 he flew 2687 hours in fifty-three different types of aircraft. Outside his initial flying training most of these flights were as the sole pilot or the captain of the aircraft. He once flew fourteen separate training flights in a Tiger Moth in one day. He flew biplanes and jets, single-engine, twin-engine and four-engine fighters, bombers and transport aircraft – British, French, American and German. He was credited with shooting down five enemy aircraft during WW2. He was awarded a Distinguished Flying Cross (DFC) in addition to his OBE; and of these achievements, in his eighty-sixth year, he remembered nothing. Yet, I had decorated his room with military aircraft pictures, aircraft he could still correctly identify; and he had recognised the sound of two Hawker Harts flying in formation sixty-two years after his last flight in one: K2125 from Hyderabad to Jodhpur on 25 March 1938, 125 minutes' flying time recorded in his log book. Even though I had lived with his progressive disability over the preceding four years, it was still incomprehensible to me.

In March 1936 he was posted from No. 2 FTS, RAF Digby, to No. 26 (Army Cooperation) Squadron based at RAF Catterick, Yorkshire where he had his first training flight in a Hawker Audax, a two-seat Hart derivative, on the 19th of that month. This flight lasted twenty minutes after which Cedric was judged competent to fly solo.

The Audax biplane was specifically designed as a two-seat army cooperation aircraft and was powered by a single, 530 horsepower, Rolls-Royce Kestrel engine. It had a maximum speed of 175 mph. It was usually armed by one fixed forward-firing machine gun operated by the pilot, and a second traversable gun operated from the rear cockpit. It could carry light bombs and other equipment under its lower wings.

Cedric's operational training at Catterick started straight away and for this he usually had an observer in the rear cockpit who operated the machine gun and performed other tasks. Part of this operational work-up included a detachment to the airfield at Old Sarum near Salisbury, Wiltshire just five miles from his final nursing home, Glenside Manor. Old Sarum later became a civilian flying club and school and it is where I started to learn to fly more than sixty years later.

In July 1936, after some forty hours of flying, Cedric was again assessed as an average pilot, and posted to No. 28 (Army Cooperation) Squadron, RAF Ambala, India. Ambala is some 150 miles due north of Delhi. The function of the squadron was to provide support to the Indian Army as it tried to suppress opposition to British colonial rule along the northern borders of India and what is now Pakistan.

On 10 November 1936 he had a fifteen-minute flight test in an Audax with Flight Lieutenant Sinclair who was to be Cedric's new flight commander in A Flt of No. 28 Squadron. He was judged proficient and started to practise operational exercises: aerial photography, gunnery, bombing, reconnaissance and message retrieval (hooked up into the aircraft as it passed over a contraption resembling a washing line). For most of these exercises he had a Leading Aircraftsman (LAC) as his observer.

In April 1937 his squadron flew north via Lahore to Manzai near to the border with Afghanistan, to support the North-West Frontier Police and later the Indian Army; his log book mentions 2nd Brigade and the Tochi Scouts, and refers to the area of operations as Waziristan. He flew operations in this area until the end of July 1937 during which time he was again assessed as an average pilot by the Officer Commanding (OC) of his squadron.

Among his papers I found a hand-written memorandum dated 3 August 1937 from him to Flight Lieutenant C.B Hughes who he addressed as OC 28 Army Cooperation Squadron (this may have been a temporary appointment as the OC of the squadron should normally have been a Squadron Leader at that time). The memo reads:

Sir,
With reference to your enquiry on my sortie with 1.0 on 27/6/37 the following are the required messages and answers

From 1.0 by R/T
09.02 Take action against enemy reported at 807862 at 08.25 25 in number

From pilot by dropping
09.30 Have inspected pinpoint only 3 encampments and 8 women seen. Am I to take action against them? (See Appendix) 09.35

From 1.0 by R/T
Enemy movement reported on ridge 805849 investigate and attack.

10.05 From pilot by dropping
Investigated ridge 805849. No enemy, 50 goats, 1 woman. Do you want action?

From 1.0

No Action

I have the honour to be Sir

Cedric A Masterman P/O

APPENDIX

The pilot did not take any action in theses cases until a thorough investigation from the air had been made. Also he did not wish to take action against non-combatants and animals outside a blockade area without permission from the ground.

In these cases permission was not granted.

Cedric's log book simply states that he flew a 2 hour, 50 minute sortie on 27 June with LAC Knowles as his observer. LAC Knowles would have been responsible for passing the messages between Cedric and the ground commander (referred to in the memorandum as '1.0')

He survived these operations in Waziristan unscathed and received recognition through a 'Mention in Despatches' (which would be indicated on his uniform medal ribbons with a small bronze oak leaf). I was unable to ascertain the reason for this recognition but I believe it may have been connected with his recognition of non-combatants described in his memorandum.

He passed his 23rd birthday back in Ambala on 25 September 1937, and flew twice on that day.

I knew that Cedric had thoroughly enjoyed his life in India as a young pilot. He captained the RAF India Rugby team and also swam competitively for the Service. He developed a strong affection for India its people and culture, learned Urdu – and had an abiding respect for Mahatma Gandhi.

The months passed pleasantly flying various Hawker Audaxes: Serial Numbers K5569, -66, -65, and -68 predominately. Occasionally he had flights in other aircraft – a Vickers Valentia twin-engine, biplane troop transport as second pilot three times, and back to a Hawker Hart in March of 1938 when his log book shows he was ferrying Captain Blunt of the Royal Engineers around Northern India.

In June 1938 the then CO of No. 28 Squadron, Squadron Leader Ward, assessed Cedric's flying ability as 'Above Average'. It had taken him 665 flying hours and 740 flights to achieve this recognition.

In February 1939, as war clouds were gathering over Europe, he was back in action on the North-West Frontier, flying from Miranshaw in support of 2 Brigade and the Tochi Scouts. On 18 May 1939 he had his last flight with No. 28 Squadron as he returned to England to start an engineering course at RAF Henlow – where I, too, was to be trained as an RAF Engineer some 27 years later.

My work in Montreal in the 1980s necessitated regular trips back to Europe every three months or so, when I usually managed to arrange a side trip to Sleaford to visit my parents. I saw my Mother for the last time just before Christmas 1988; two weeks later Cedric phoned me in Canada to say that she had died. I and Ruth flew back to England on New Year's Eve for the funeral. While there I spoke to Pat Whitelaw, the lady who cleaned my parents' bungalow, and she agreed to go to the house each day to see that Cedric was alright and prepare food for him. He was physically fit and seemingly mentally alert at this time, and had a dog to keep him company and to take on walks. He also had a large circle of friends in Sleaford who agreed to look out for him and to apprise me of any serious problems with his well being. I had no compunction in leaving him to return to Canada.

Cedric's social life then was centred round the local pubs and clubs, as it had been for many years. Each morning he would dress himself in a smart suit and take his dog Jumble, a Munsterlander, for a long walk by the River Slea. Then, promptly at 11 a.m., he would walk the five minutes into town to shop. He bought a newspaper to read in the afternoon and then went to the butcher, baker and other shops where he purchased, as a minimum I found out later, two lamb chops, small cakes and sometimes a kipper. He then went to three pubs drinking a pint of beer in each. Returning home, he would put his food purchases into the fridge and then eat cold food that Pat had prepared for him. In the evening, he would get in his car and drive to the Sleaford Rugby, Soccer or Cricket clubs where he would pass the evening drinking beer and helping with committee work usually as Treasurer. On returning home he would again eat some cold food prepared by Pat, watch the television news at 9 p.m, for half an hour, and then retire to bed. He never cooked the lamb chops (Pat cooked them for him) or anything else for himself. It never seemed to occur to him to eat out by himself, although when I visited he was always very keen to visit one of the local Indian restaurants – I always paid.

Jumble died a few months after my Mother; Cedric claimed he still went for what he called a 'dog-less dog walk' each morning, but with the benefit of hindsight I think that was probably just in his imagination.

And so this life of his continued for a few years. Every Sunday morning he would phone me in Canada – he never grasped the time difference and the call usually came through at 5 a.m. Eventually Ruth rebelled and unplugged the phone every Saturday night – I would then phone him as soon as I got up on Sunday.

I saw Cedric every four months or so during the three years following my Mother's death. Pat urged me to see him more often. She hinted that she was having problems with him: he wouldn't let her throw any newspapers away, claiming that he hadn't read them, and the fridge gradually got fuller and fuller with uneaten lamb chops, kippers and cakes – each time I visited I threw everything out.

On one visit I saw that part of the low brick wall separating the bungalow's front garden from the road had been demolished. Cedric explained that a delivery vehicle had backed into it a few days before and its owners were about to make repairs. On my next visit the wall was exactly as before with debris still littering the garden. Cedric again said that a delivery vehicle had backed into it a few days before and that the owners were about to make repairs, but he was unable to tell me who the owners were. I located a local builder who agreed to make the repairs when he had time. I returned to Canada. During a phone call with Pat about a month later she told me that the wall still hadn't been repaired. I phoned the builder who told me that when he had gone with men and materials to rebuild the wall Cedric had turned them away, saying that the delivery van's owners had just agreed to repair the wall and were about to start. It was all fiction of course, although he genuinely believed that what he was saying was true. The wall lay broken for another two years or so until I finally managed to arrange for its repair.

At about the same time the saga of the house subsidence started. The interior of the house had been left untouched since the death of my mother. Pat kept it spotless, but everything had to remain in exactly the same place as the day my mother died.

While there for a short stay, I looked up in the lounge and noticed a hairline crack across the ceiling; Cedric said that it had always been like that. Over the next two years it widened to a six inch gap and ran down one of the exterior walls of the room. I urged him to get it seen to, but he didn't. I tried cajoling him, asking him what my house-proud mother would have thought of her house now, but to no end. The garden was also becoming messy but I managed to engage a gardener to cut the grass and generally tidy things up when necessary. Cedric didn't object to that because my mother used to have occasional gardening help; but how this new gardener was being paid Cedric had no idea. However, still he did nothing about the damaged house.

By now it was clear that I owed Cedric closer supervision than I could provide from Canada. I enquired about getting him accepted into Canada as a dependent but was told that with his apparently deteriorating mental state he would not meet the medical criteria for immigration. I asked the multi-national company I worked for in Montreal if I could have a transfer to Europe; the company, Ruth and my two, by now grown-up and totally independent, daughters agreed.

3

Westland Lysander

Germany invaded Poland on 1 September 1939 and Britain declared war on Germany two days later.

No flying is recorded in Cedric's log book between his last No. 28 Squadron Audax flight and a solo flight in a Queen Bee on 18 September 1939. The Queen Bee was built by De Havilland as a gunnery target adaptation of the famous Tiger Moth two seat biplane. Queen Bees were owned by the Royal Navy and some, at least, were fitted with a radio-controlled automatic pilot. The log book recalls that the flight was from Weyborne to Henlow; this makes sense as Weyborne, in Norfolk, was still a practice area for ground to air gunnery for many years after the war, and Henlow was where Cedric was taking his engineering training.

On 21 September Cedric made a flight by himself in a Miles Magister – a small monoplane trainer (see Chapter 5*)* – and on 6

October in a Hawker Hind, two-seat light bomber and trainer, yet another Hart derivative. By 13 October, however, his engineering training had been cancelled and he was making his first flight in a Westland Lysander at RAF Odiham, Hampshire, as a Flight Commander (he was by now a Flight Lieutenant) of No. 225 Squadron. This flight lasted just thirty minutes and was his only practical training on the type. His instructor that day was Flight Lieutenant Stickley, who had been in No. 28 Squadron in India with him and was to remain a firm friend of his for many years.

The Lysander was a high-wing monoplane specifically designed as an army cooperation aircraft. It had a fixed, tail-wheel undercarriage, was powered by a single Bristol Mercury or Perseus rotary piston engine of about 850 horsepower, carried an observer in addition to the single pilot but had room for more passengers in an emergency. In addition to its observer-operated machine gun, the aircraft could carry a useful bomb load on racks attached to the main undercarriage. The wing was aerodynamically quite sophisticated with high-lift devices that permitted very short take-offs and landings. The stalling speed was also low, but flying the Lysander slowly required skill and respect as it sometimes lured pilots into stalls near the ground with fatal results. It was never a great success in its original army cooperation role, but came into its own as a special-duties communications aircraft flying clandestine missions at night behind enemy lines – many agents were put into German-occupied Europe from Britain by Lysander crews.

The photograph shows the aircraft that Cedric usually flew; in his war-time photo album he calls it 'My Aircraft – Old Faithful'. His observer was usually Pilot Officer Warner.

On 10 November 1939 his flying ability was assessed as above average as a pilot by his Squadron Commander; an assessment that was repeated for the remainder of his flying career.

On 18 November he had his first, and only, significant flying accident when a Lysander flown by him (not Old Faithful) blew a tyre on take-off and turned upside down as a result, leaving Cedric with a damaged ankle. This injury does not seem to have prevented him from flying because his log book shows he was flying Lysanders again two days later.

Later that November, while he seemingly

was attached to the Royal Navy shore station HMS Raven for a few days, he made several solo flights in a Fairy Battle.

The Battle was a very much larger and more powerful aircraft than any he had flown previously but, as so often in his career, Cedric seems to have just arrived at this totally new and unfamiliar aircraft, climbed in and flown it by himself. It was a monoplane, daylight medium bomber powered by a single Rolls-Royce Merlin engine producing about 1000 horsepower; its maximum speed was 250 mph. In addition to one pilot it carried an observer/bomb-aimer and a radio operator/gunner. First deliveries to the RAF started in 1937 and by the outbreak of war 1000 examples had been delivered. It was very lightly armed and its first encounters with German fighters and ground defences were disastrous, particularly if – as was usual – no fighter escort was provided; in one 1940 daylight bombing raid 35 out of 63 Battles failed to return. Battles were withdrawn from active operations later that year and relegated to training, target towing and experimental duties in which they served well.

In December 1939 – this was still very much the quiet period of WW2 for the

French and British before the storm and known as the 'Phoney War' – Cedric was somewhere in France where he flew a Spad – a French biplane fighter – which he noted in his log book as *'Aircraft belonging to 15th Escadrille. Very nice machine equal to the Gladiator'*. The Gloucester Gladiator biplane fighter of the RAF was still in service at the beginning of WW2 and served with distinction in Malta and Norway (see Chapter 4).

He later flew from England via France as a passenger/co-pilot in civil transport aircraft to Oran, Algeria (then part of French North Africa) where he somehow acquired a Lysander which he flew around several French military bases there. He was also allowed to fly a French Caudron C-620 'Simoun' (Sandstorm), a light, 4-seat transport aircraft, in the company of a French Colonel. His log book gives no clue as to why he spent most of December 1939 commuting between England, France and Algeria.

By the end of January 1940 Cedric was back at Odiham with No. 225 Squadron and for the next four months his flying entirely comprised air exercises in Lysanders.

My company had no aeronautical position

in mainland UK to match my expertise but did have a suitable opening in its Belfast, Northern Ireland facility. Ruth and I flew to Belfast to see how we might like to live there. We travelled with some foreboding as the sectarian troubles there were still in full swing; however, we liked what we saw, found a house and in early 1992 moved from Montreal.

My work involved a great deal of travel to England and so I was able to see Cedric much more often than before. I found a consulting civil engineer who agreed to look at the apparent subsidence of Cedric's house. He and I went to the house together – Cedric raised no objection – and he determined that the subsidence was being caused by a broken water pipe beneath the house foundations which was causing underpinnings to wash away. He said it was all fixable but the necessary work would take about ten days to effect including the making good of the decorations in the lounge.

Cedric, I predicted, would not accept a troop of workmen digging up his house so I asked him to visit me in Belfast for two weeks – my 50th birthday was coming up in June 1992 – and he enthusiastically agreed. The civil engineer found a contractor who guaranteed not only to complete the work within ten days of starting, but also to restore the decoration to exactly the way it had been before the damage started.

Cedric made his own arrangements to fly to Belfast from Luton airport. He spent his two weeks with Ruth and me, and returned to a fully restored house. I phoned him when he got home to enquire after his journey and innocently ask about the cracks in the lounge ceilings and walls. 'What cracks?' was his response. 'This house is perfect, just as your Mother left it.' Pat later confirmed that the contractor had done a marvellous job – and had repaired the garden wall. I paid his bill.

Cedric enjoyed most of his time in Belfast. Our house was in a quiet neighbourhood near the shore of Belfast Lough, and there was a path directly from the house to the local pub. Ruth was not working full time then and was content to run Cedric around in her car and take him for walks with our dog. I took him out to a pub each evening, as was his usual routine. I showed him the ten-minute walk to the local pub and, on his second day, Ruth sent him to walk by himself for his pre-lunch beers. He came back on our friendly milkman's electric milk float; the milkman had found him wandering lost by the shores of the lough. This happened twice more after which solo walks were banned.

He also got lost in Belfast. Ruth and I had to go into the city to be fitted with new reading glasses. Cedric didn't want to wait inside the opticians; instead he would, he said, wait outside and look at the buildings (which were, indeed, very fine). He was separated from us for no more than five minutes, but in that time wandered off and was nowhere to be seen. We searched the shopping core of Belfast city but no Cedric. Eventually, we enquired at the central police station – a very imposing building surrounded by armed guards and anti-mortar fencing. 'Oh, you must be Christopher Masterman,' I was told after explaining that I had lost my father. 'He's just been here looking for you. He had no idea where you lived but he said that you were an executive with the Short Brothers, so we phoned them up and they gave us your address. He's just being run home now.'

When we got home, there was a police car with smiling policemen and Cedric standing by, all waiting for us to turn up with the house key. We kept a better eye on him after that.

It had now become clear through our first-hand experiences that Cedric was developing a bad problem with his memory or lack thereof. Ruth, who was a nurse, started to read up on age-related dementia and passed relevant articles onto me. The symptoms we were observing matched those of early Alzheimer's. What we had witnessed so far had all been fairly benign, amusing really, and some articles recommended that we treat such incidents as humorous and be ready to laugh at them as a remedy to the frustrations that might in future follow. We knew that we had a problem, and it was likely to get worse, much worse; but we had no way of knowing the pace of subsequent deterioration and how incapacitating the illness might become, or of predicting its effects on our lives.

I entered a kind of denial. Cedric was suffering from a bad memory, nothing worse. After all, he looked after his own financial affairs, dressed well, still drove competently, and was socially adept – no stranger holding a conversation with him would ever have guessed that whole episodes from his life were beginning to get away from him. For several years to come friends would tell us that they could detect nothing wrong with him. Ruth's reading on Alzheimer's disease also predicted some character changes that would not seem as benign as the simple, funny, memory-loss incidents we had witnessed so far. We did not have long to wait for the first more serious episode.

4

Gloucester Gladiator

In early 1940 both sides of the WW2 conflict decided to land forces in Norway. Germany wanted, among other considerations, to gain fortress-like anchorages for its heavy warships in the Norwegian fords from where they could attack British shipping. This prospect was of serious concern to the British government which also wanted to block German access to Swedish iron ore. In great haste, an Allied expeditionary force was assembled to land in Norway; this force was known as X Force.

On 9 April 1940 the Germans invaded Denmark and Norway. Denmark capitulated almost immediately under threat of Copenhagen being bombed, but Norway, with its rugged topography and few roads, was a tougher proposition. Germany mounted land, sea and air assaults on southern and central Norway and was immediately attacked by the Royal Navy which succeeded in inflicting heavy damage on the German fleet. However, the German invasion was successful and secured the lower portion of Norway for the Reich.

British and French troops started to land on the central and northern portions of the Norwegian coast on 14 April and joined with local forces that were still trying to stem the German advances. These actions collectively became known as the Narvik campaign; it proved a failure and only a few weeks after landing in Norway the Allied forces had to be evacuated after suffering heavy losses during the campaign and subsequent withdrawal.

On 22 April 1940 as Cedric was sitting, probably bored, in the officers' mess at Odiham, he was asked if he would like to go to Norway. He leapt at the opportunity to do something other than air exercise in a Lysander (or at least, I imagine so), and drove up to the Air Ministry in London the next day. There he met Wing Commander Maxton who was to be his temporary boss, but he was given no other information on his mission other than that he was to travel to Scotland.

On 23 April he flew from RAF Hendon, on the northern outskirts of London, to

Invergordon, Scotland in a De Havilland Flamingo, twin-engine, transport aircraft with Maxton, Flying Officer Ball and five RAF radio operators. There, to his disbelief, he was told by Maxton that he and the other members of his party would be flying to Namsos, a town approximately halfway up the western coast of Norway, to construct landing grounds for the RAF elements of X Force. Namsos was one of the major landing places for X Force and was under severe siege by the Germans.

I found a great deal of material about Cedric's experiences in Norway among his personal effects, including a transcript of his diary. In 1978 he had been contacted by Knut Store, a Norwegian Air force Officer, who was seeking information about his role in Norway. Cedric did some extensive research and then wrote a graphic account of his time with X Force which I used as a basis for this chapter, and for his published obituary.

The party boarded an RAF Shorts Sunderland, four-engine, flying boat on the evening of 24 April, and at 5 a.m the next morning they found themselves flying over Namsos, which had been severely damaged by German bombing. The aircraft set down on the adjacent fjord which was crowded with British and French warships and their support vessels. The aircraft moored next to HMS *Calcutta,* an anti-aircraft cruiser, to which Cedric and his companions transferred. There he met three Luftwaffe prisoners; his account written for Knut reads:

In my diary I have written: 'Three airmen prisoners aboard, very young, pleasant lads, pity this war is knocking off lads like these.' *I wonder if they were true words. I doubt it; now my opinion has changed a great deal.*

The next day Cedric's party was moved to hutted accommodation ashore. From then until 2 May Cedric witnessed the destruction of Namsos and the sinking of several Allied ships by the Luftwaffe. It proved impossible to build any airstrips, or even find suitable terrain for them, not only because of the continuous air attacks but also because of the lack of suitable maps, deep snow on the ground and an understandable reluctance on the part of the locals to lend active help for fear of reprisals once, as they thought inevitable (and correctly), the German ground forces arrived to take the town. Instead, the RAF contingent salvaged guns from crashed aircraft and used them to help defend the town against the Luftwaffe.

On 2 May the order was given for the general evacuation of X Force from the Namsos area. Cedric and his party boarded HMS *Carlisle,* a sister ship to HMS *Calcutta,* for withdrawal back to Scotland. They were to be transferred later to the destroyer HMS *Alfridi,* but this move was delayed as *Alfridi* was seemingly being singled out for Luft-waffe attack. In his account Cedric encap-sulated his thoughts on leaving Namsos as follows:

During the afternoon I saw my last raid on Namsos; its duration was not long neither was it serious. The guns fired as usual and the railway train came in (Cedric's name for the sound of sticks of bombs falling from aircraft to the ground) *and, rather surprisingly, a Jerry went down. Poor Namsos, such wanton destruction by the enemy I had not seen up to that time. Despite this town being a military objective on account of the stores and equipment there, I was genuinely pained to see it razed to the ground. Not a house stood in the main town, there was no distinguish-ing between road or street blocks, all were on the same level and equally morbid to the sight. There just remained the North and East walls of the church, which now stood sentinel of the organised destruction and unequalled brutality of as modern civilization – Nazi Germany in all her vile and loathsome glory.*

I only waited to see the Chasseur Alpine (crack French troops) *go past, it made me sick at heart; never before had I seen a withdrawal under these conditions. They were splendid men, and looked every bit as their last war record had made them, with sunken eyes and feverishly red faces they dragged their feet behind them as though sleep walking. One could see that sheer fatigue would soon overcome them, but not one scrap of equipment had they lost, not even the skis which they now carried across their packs.*

The convoy of ships, which included HMS *Carlisle,* came under intense attack as it evacuated the fjord; HMS *Alfridi* was sunk before his eyes. He arrived in Scapa Flow, North of Scotland, at 4 a.m. on 5 May, where he learned that he would shortly be returning to Norway to try again to build airstrips, this time at Bodø which was about 200 miles up the coast from Namsos. He transferred from HMS *Carlisle* to the *Duchess of Atholl,* a 20,000-ton troop ship from the Canadian Pacific steamship fleet, and waited while a new convoy of ships was assembled.

On 10 May 1940 Germany attacked France and the Low Countries. That same day Cedric and his party sailed out of Scapa Flow en route for Bodø where they arrived on the evening of 13 May to help in the continued evacuation of Norway. The unloading of equipment and personnel from the evacuation convoy started immediately as did reconnoitring for a suitable airfield site and engagement of local resources to build it. Cedric remained on the ship until 16 May by which time shore billets had been found for all of the RAF personnel.

The airstrip was built between 14 and 25 May. It was crudely constructed of wire-mesh-covered turf sods – some 160,000 of them – and measured approximately 50 yards wide by 700 yards long. At the same time splinter-proof shelters were constructed for the expected aircraft along with bomb shelters for RAF personnel, flight offices and an officers' mess. Telephone and electrical cables were laid. At one stage 200 men were working night and day along with 75 horses and carts. All this went on under occasional attacks by the Luftwaffe. During one of these attacks, Cedric reported, three soldiers were killed and twelve other men wounded – some of whom may have been members of the locally contracted work-force.

On 26 May three Gloucester Gladiators flew onto the new airstrip from No. 263 Squadron's operational base at Bardufoss to the north of Narvik about 100 miles away. The Gladiators' task was to provide air cover as the withdrawal of X Force and Norwegian forces from Norway continued. The three pilots – Flight Lieutenant Hull, Pilot Officer Falkson and Lieutenant Lydekker had all volunteered for this task. Lieutenant Lydekker was a Royal Navy pilot who had been transferred from his original No. 804 Squadron RN to No. 263 Squadron RAF as a replacement for casualties.

All of this was going on as the evacuation of British expeditionary troops along with some French, Dutch and Belgian forces from France to England began – the 'miracle' of Dunkirk.

The Gloucester Gladiator was the last of the RAF's biplane fighters and the first with a totally enclosed cockpit. Even as it entered service in 1937 it was already obsolescent; nevertheless, because neither of its two monoplane successors – Hurricane and Spitfire – had then entered series production, it was ordered in quantity as a stopgap for both the RAF and the RN. It was powered by an 830-horsepower Bristol radial engine, was armed with four forward-firing machine guns and had a top speed in level flight of 250 mph. It thus compared poorly, on paper, with not only the German monoplane fighters it would be up against but also some of the German bombers. However, its record in combat was to belie, to some extent, its performance shortcomings.

When the Gladiators landed, all three became bogged down. They were extricated and moved to the airstrip's firmest area which measured 300 yards long, just sufficient for the aircraft to operate from – which they did after refuelling. Later that day 300 yards of wooden snowboards were laid over the sods to provide a better surface.

In looking through Cedric's documents I found several accounts of the Gladiators' unequal battle with the Luftwaffe in the skies above Bodø; the clearest account came from Bodø itself and was probably compiled by Knut Store – it is reproduced in part below.

After an hour's flying (from Bardufoss) *the*

Gladiators landed in Bodø and all three aircraft became stuck in the soft ground. Whilst two of the planes refuelled, Lieutenant Lydekker was sent up to patrol the airfield. Just as the (other two) *planes were ready for flight, two He 111s* (German Heinkel twin-engine medium bombers) *suddenly appeared. Hull and Falkson took off immediately, but Falkson crashed during take-off as a result of the poor airstrip. Lydekker, who in the meantime had chased the Heinkels, was instructed by Hull to land and remain there. Hull himself flew to Saltdalen in accordance with Wing Commander Maxton's instructions, to cover his own force which was constantly being attacked by German planes. Over Saltdalen Hull saw a He 111 he shot down. After this, another He 111 and Ju 52* (German Junkers three-engine transport aircraft) *appeared. The Heinkel escaped whilst the Junkers was an easy target for the experienced Briton. Two other Heinkels turned and disappeared to the South. A further two Ju 52s were too late to escape, one vanished into the clouds with a tail of smoke after him, whilst the other was seen spinning helplessly to the ground. The last plane Hull engaged in battle was an He 111. This was fired upon until he had no more ammunition. Its fate is unknown.*

Thanks to Hull's efforts, the Irish Guards and

the Norwegian Company Ellinger were able to withdraw towards Rognan without being attacked by German planes.

On his way back to Bodø Hull met a formation of Ju 88s. He managed to split them up and landed at 5 p.m. At 5.30 p.m. he was away again in the air on his way to Saltdalen. No German planes were to be seen so Hull entertained the ground forces with a display of air acrobatics! For the rest of the evening and night until 4.30 a.m. the three pilots took turns patrolling the Rognan area during the evacuation of 2000 British and Norwegian troops. After this they held watch with one aircraft.

At 8 o'clock on the morning of the 27th, the airfield at Bodø was attacked by 12 Ju 87s (the infamous 'Stuka' dive bombers) escorted by 4 ME 110s (German Messerschmitt Bf 110 twin-engine, long-range fighter bomber). Lydekker took off at once but Hull was unable to start his aircraft. He took cover nearby and when he saw that the attack was not directed against the airfield itself he started up and took off without taking the time to fasten his harness or parachute. He immediately attacked and inflicted damage to a Ju 87 which flew off to the South. He was then attacked by another Stuka and was hit by a bullet in the knee, whilst another grazed his head. He lost consciousness for a moment, and after coming to himself again he crash-landed at Skagodden, from where he was taken to hospital. Lydekker fought on against heavy odds, damaged a Ju 87, and as he thought Hull was still at Bodø, he decided to fly to Bardufoss. His plane was severely damaged and written off, Lydekker himself was also wounded in the neck and shoulder and was sent to hospital.

Later in the evening of the 27th, during the bombing of Bodø, Pilot Officer Falkson showed great courage whilst driving an ambulance to assist in the evacuation of Bodø hospital.

Cedric's notes of the events at Bodø contain a graphic description of the German attacks on the airfield and town.

1800hrs, 12 Ju 87 and 4 Me 110 attacked airfield and made a devil of a mess of it. I was in the bottom of the new prison at the time; I was in a pretty flat spin because the masonry was falling down and these big chaps (meaning big bombs) feel damned close even at 150–200 yards. Afterwards I went out to see if all the boys (i.e. his men) were OK; they were but they had taken a pretty hefty machine gunning. After ten minutes we heard the drone of engines again and then I ran for a ditch just off the airfield;

55

somehow I have a great fear of air-raid shelters
although I made some beauties for the men and
they stood up to the task. It was just a matter of
seconds before the first bomb dropped; all
bombing was done in stick fashion and was
horrid. The hospital was the first place to get a
crack and went straight up in flames. Next the
town was systematically razed to the ground.
The machine gunning was wicked and amid
bomb blasts and the scream of bullets I prayed as
I have never prayed before. I was wet through
with icy water and terrified in the ditch. I
collected Wick (Mr E.Wik, the Norwegian
civil engineer locally engaged to build the
airfield) *and an 18-yr-old airman and we*
made our way towards the town not realising
what was happening there. After an hour or
more we were faced with two hundred yards of
open ground to cover, so I decided to wait in the
water; why we did not freeze I cannot imagine.
When the fury had abated we dashed to RAF
HQ where we arrived exhausted and as pale as
sheets. The lads were great and before long I was
dry and changed sucking a bottle of beer. Then
the wounded from the hospital came pouring in
and we turned the place into a clearing station.
The nurses were wonderful and Doc. Scott did
his stuff splendidly. Amongst the men were two
women about to have infants, so I dashed off to

the Navy and collected a bottle of rum; we gave the girls one each apiece all round and shared the rest among ourselves. At this time Maxton was missing and as we believed had gone. But after some hours he turned up and had proved to be helping in the hospital; he was there visiting Hull when the raid commenced. Later the sergeant turned up with all men; it is amazing how they got away. Those in the shelters were safe enough except from direct stuff but many were in the open like myself.

Attacks on Bodø continued as Allied troops congregated awaiting evacuation. The airfield could not be repaired so Cedric and his party waited amid rumour and counter-rumour for the arrival of ships to take them back to Britain, hopefully before they could be captured by the advancing Germans. At the same time that Norway was being evacuated so was another British army driven to the seas by advancing German forces – at Dunkirk

Cedric's men left Bodø for Borkenes on a destroyer on 7 June; from there they were transferred to a troop ship convoy and returned safely to the UK. Cedric's notes do not record his journey back to the UK although it can be inferred that he left a day or two after his men. However, his notes include these last recollections of Bodø:

It was a pitiful sight and the stench of burning human flesh still rings home in my brain. Not a thing stands in Bodø, the church, hospital hotel, everything is gone; just a few chimneys stand sentinel as monuments to the cremated – women and children, victims of a violence that can strike at our own homes. (Prophetic words as the aerial blitz of Britain had not yet started.)

The three brave Gladiator pilots also left Bodø. But Pilot Officer Falkson was killed when the aircraft carrier HMS *Glorious,* which was conveying the men and machines of Nos. 46 and 263 squadrons away from Norway, was caught and sunk by the two German warships *Scharnhorst* and *Gneisenau* with great loss of life.

Lieutenant Lydekker died on 15 November 1942 when the aircraft carrier HMS *Avenger* was sunk by a German submarine off the coast of Africa; there were only twelve survivors from the ship's complement of 550.

Flight Lieutenant Hull (newly promoted to Squadron Leader) was shot down and killed on 7 September 1940 over the River Thames Estuary during the Battle of Britain.

Cedric was awarded the Order of the British Empire (OBE) in the 1941 New Years Honours List. This would have been a very unusual acknowledgement of his part in the Norway campaign as it is not awarded for gallantry or, usually, for single acts of outstanding service. A twenty-six year old RAF pilot would have been a very rare recipient of the OBE, particularly in wartime.

In 1977 the Norwegian Air Force and Citizens of Bodø honoured the memory of the three Gladiator pilots with a stone monument near the site of the airfield that Cedric had helped to build. The inscription reads:

'On the 26 of May 1940, three Gloucester Gladiator fighter aircraft of No. 263 Squadron landed on a temporary airstrip near Bodø. Unfalteringly the pilots of these aircraft challenged a numerically superior adversary and inflicted great loss upon the enemy. Later, they gave their lives for freedom. This memorial is erected in their honour.'

Cedric visited Bodø in 1979 with my mother. He was warmly welcomed by Knut Store and other citizens, and he met up again with the Norwegian civil engineer, Mr E.Wik.

I visited Bodø with Ruth for just four hours in 2001, after Cedric had died; it was a stopping point for the ship in which we were cruising up the Norwegian coast. I was hosted by Knut who showed me around the Norwegian Air Force museum which was built very close to where the temporary airstrip had been. He was also able to show me the ditch in which Cedric had sheltered on 27 May 1940, and told me that Engineer Wik was still hale and hearty.

My 50th birthday arrived while Cedric was in Belfast. He recognised it as an important milestone for me and said that he would treat Ruth and me to dinner. We hadn't booked anywhere so opted for a local inn which we knew from previous experience had good, hearty but inexpensive pub fare. We ordered drinks while we studied the simple, single-page menu – Cedric had his usual pint of beer as did I. I asked him what he fancied from the half a dozen or so choices: fish & chips, steaks and other grills, and pasta were the mainstays. The prices were reasonable.

'Well,' he said. 'I'm not having anything

from this menu, it's all far too expensive.'

I gently pointed out that each dish was little more than twice the price of the pint of beer in front of him – for which I had paid even though it was my birthday treat.

'I don't care,' he replied, and with his voice rising to a shout 'I'm not paying those prices, she (pointing to Ruth) can cook us something at home.' I looked at him, quickly finished my beer, and took us all home.

By the time the ten-minute journey was complete he had calmed down. As we walked in the door of the house he said 'I'm sorry that I didn't want to eat in that place, but you must agree the prices were terrible.'

I said that Ruth and I were going out to eat by ourselves, and would leave him in the house with a sandwich. He started to weep, repeating again and again how sorry he was. Ruth broke first – I was still very angry – and said he could come if he promised to behave himself. She whispered to me that she would pay, and we wouldn't show Cedric the menu.

She remembered that a new Indian restaurant had opened in the next village. As we went through the door Cedric asked what was going on. I said that we were going to buy him a nice Indian meal. 'Oh, good,' he said. 'What's the occasion? Is it my birthday?'

On his first day with us in Belfast I had lectured Cedric not to tell anyone that he had served in the RAF, and – in particular – never to mention that I had also been a British serviceman. He seemed to understand the importance and reasons. But, on his return to Sleaford, he had sent me a thankyou note through the post addressed to 'Squadron Leader C.S.Masterman RAF Retired', fortunately without any consequences to me.

He didn't visit us in Belfast again but I continued to see him every two months or so when my work took me to England; he seemed to be coping with his life.

5

Miles Magister

Italy declared war on France and Britain on 10 June 1940 – thereby siding with Germany, its fellow 'Axis' power since 1936.

Paris fell to the Germans on 14 June. On 23 June France was forced to sign an armistice with Germany, and two days later with Italy. Soon it was to be Great Britain's turn for concentrated German attention

On 19 June Cedric, newly promoted to Squadron Leader, was back flying a Lysander with No. 225 Squadron which by now was operating from RAF Chitterne in Wiltshire, south-west England. On the same day he took up a Percival Proctor for the first time with an old friend from No. 28 Squadron, Flight Lieutenant Richard Rhys, as his co-pilot (Richard later became our family solicitor). The Proctor was a 3- or 4-seat light communications and radio training monoplane powered by a single 210 horsepower De Havilland Gypsy Queen, 6-cylinder, in-line piston engine.

On 20 July Cedric was on a reconnaissance flight over the south coast of England when he came across a group of 24 JU 87 Stuka dive bombers; they were probably looking for ground-based targets to soften up prior to the start of what was to become known as The Battle of Britain. Cedric's Lysander would have been no match for 24 Stukas (although they were very vulnerable to fighter aircraft), so presumably he took evasive action and made his retreat back to Odiham. The aerial war over England was about to hot up, and Cedric was not taking a proactive role in it. This must have been immensely frustrating to him, particularly after witnessing the destruction of Namsos and Bodø, but greater frustration was to come.

The usually accepted duration of the Battle of Britain, when the air defences of Britain were so nearly defeated by the German Luftwaffe – a defeat that would have opened the way to Operation 'Sea Lion' and the invasion of the UK – was between 12 August and 30 September 1940. During this critical period of the war, Cedric's RAF contemporaries were flying their Spitfires and Hurricanes over the southern half of

England and desperately trying to turn back the Luftwaffe onslaught on, first, the radar towers, then the fighter airfields and, finally, London. Many of these pilots were already close friends of Cedric, or later became so, and some were killed. Cedric, however, had no part in any of this: he was flying his Lysander on mundane photographic, bombing or air firing practices although there were also some patrols over the English Channel; he must have felt frustrated.

On 8 September he stopped even this flying until the end of October. Cedric's log book gives no clue as to what he was doing during this highly critical period in the RAF's history. He surely would not have felt comfortable on the ground, particularly after his experiences of being bombed and strafed in Norway. His subsequent record shows he was a fighter, and a highly effective one. He would have wanted to be taking on the Luftwaffe in a front-line fighter – but in late 1940 he had never flown anything faster than the 250 mph Fairy Battle.

The RAF was expanding fast, new aircraft were streaming off production lines but there was a critical shortage of pilots. Flying training was therefore given a high priority and new flying schools were established both in Britain and in its colonies and dominions. Thus, it is no surprise that Cedric's log book entry for 29 October 1940 shows he was training to be an elementary flying instructor flying De Havilland Tiger Moths and Miles Magisters.

The Tiger Moth was a fabric-covered, two-seat, elementary training biplane. It was powered by a 130 horsepower De Havilland Gypsy Major engine similar to the Gypsy Queen engine of the Proctor. It had started life as a successful civil aircraft and then modified for military use. Some 6000 examples were built mainly in the UK and Canada but also by Norway, Portugal and Sweden. Some were fitted with bomb racks with the idea that they could be used in last-ditch defence of the UK if Germany had invaded; as the total aircraft bomb load was just eight 20-pound bombs it is unlikely that this 'Dad's Air Force' would have had much effect on any invaders. The Tiger Moth was to become one of Cedric's favourite aircraft and he flew examples literally hundreds of times during and after WW2.

Although the Miles Magister shared no lineage with the Tiger Moth, it can be succinctly described as a wood-covered monoplane version of the latter, and the power plant was essentially identical. It proved to be an excellent training aircraft and, being considerably faster than the Tiger Moth (maximum of 156 mph versus 109 mph) was also popular for other roles – many RAF squadrons had one on strength for general duties (or, unofficially, as the Commanding Officer's personal transport).

Cedric's log book shows that his flying instructor training took place at No. 4 SFIS (Senior Flight Instructor School) which was located near Cambridge. After 16 hours of flight training he was assessed as above average for both flying and instructor abilities. He was now a qualified flying instructor and on 11 November 1940 he rejoined No. 225 Squadron in its Training Flight.

For the next few months Cedric taught *ab initio* pilots, flying up to six sorties with them almost every day. The Magister was the aircraft used mostly, but his log book also shows flights in Tiger Moths and Proctors.

Fourteen flights in a Miles Minor are also recorded during November and December 1940 and January 1941. These flights were all very short – typically five minutes with the longest just fifteen minutes – and annotated as test flights with some, at least, taking place at 'A&E'. My research showed that the Miles M.30 X Minor was a small, twin-engine, one-off experimental aircraft, designed to evaluate the characteristics of blended fuselage and wing intersections. RAF Chitterne, which was then Cedric's home base, is near to RAF Boscombe Down – then as now the British centre for test and evaluation of aircraft and aircraft armaments – and the department there at that time responsible for aircraft evaluation was called A&E. It seems that Cedric was moonlighting as a part-time test pilot!

On 11 February 1941 he and my mother, Cynthia, were married and he seems to have been on leave for the period 4 to 14 February, as no flying is recorded for those two weeks.

Towards the end of February Cedric was posted for several weeks to No. 13 Squadron, RAF Hooton Park – an airfield on the outskirts of Liverpool. There he helped to rebuild this Lysander squadron which had fared badly when in France. He continued his training responsibilities using Lysanders in addition to Magisters, Tiger Moths and Proctors.

In 1994, two years after my 50th birthday, my Canadian company asked me to move from Belfast to help run a company in England that they had just purchased. I was reluctant to go as Ruth and I were happily settled in Northern Ireland, and I wasn't sure that I would fit in with the culture of this other organisation. However, my managing director made me an offer that I couldn't refuse so we moved from the shores of Belfast Lough to a large old, thatched cottage called 'Orchards' in the New Forest of southern England. Cedric was then 80 years of age and still living in Sleaford under the watchful eyes of Pat and his many local friends. He was some 200 miles from my new home and not far from a major client of mine so I was able to visit him more frequently. Ruth and I also occasionally visited his three surviving, widowed sisters: Noeleen just outside of Wolverhampton, Joan in Cambridge, and Joyce in North London. All three were older than Cedric; a fourth sister, Chrissie, had been the oldest of all but had died some years previously having shown signs of dementia.

Cedric was still driving his very battered Ford Cortina estate wagon. This car was the end marker of his long line of cars which had included Aston Martin, Mercedes-Benz, Audi and Alfa Romeo. The Ford had been bought years before as a second car solely to transport his dogs, but in the end outlasted all his desire for high-priced motoring toys. It wasn't that he could no longer afford exotica, he just wasn't interested in them any more. This was just as well because, although his driving skills remained good, he completely neglected any maintenance of his last vehicle, and it is likely that only that Ford could have withstood such treatment without complaint. Every once in a while he drove to spend a few days with each of his sisters, all of whom were less than three hours from him by road.

One Saturday Ruth and I drove north from the New Forest to visit her relatives in Staffordshire. Noeleen's house was on the way so we dropped in to see her, and also Cedric who was spending the same weekend with her. There was no sign of Cedric's car outside Noeleen's house. I asked her when Cedric was supposed to arrive. Noeleen replied 'Oh, he has already been here – you have missed him'.

'I thought he was staying the weekend with you?' I queried.

'That's right', she replied. 'I looked out of the window when he was about due (you know how his timing is always perfect) and saw him drive past. That was about three hours ago, perhaps he's gone straight to the pub.'

Just then the phone rang and was answered in the kitchen by Noeleen as she was preparing tea. She came into the lounge with the tea tray. 'That was your father,' she said to me. 'He's just arrived back in Sleaford and thanked me for a lovely visit!'

Joan asked Cedric to spend Christmas with her in Cambridge the same year. Cambridge is an easy journey from Sleaford and wouldn't have taken him much more than an hour to drive. He was to stay with her from Christmas Eve until after New Year's Day. I had already seen him in Sleaford just before Christmas.

On 27 December Joan phoned me. She said that Cedric was driving her mad with his forgetfulness, that she wanted him to leave but his car wouldn't start. I spoke to him to ask what the matter was with the car – he couldn't say, in fact he denied the car wouldn't start and refused to call a local garage for help. The weather wasn't good – cold with snow showers – but I decided to drive the four hours or so up to Cambridge to see what I could do to help. I took some tools and battery jumper leads, and made my way up to and around London then onto the Cambridge road.

It was about 7 p.m. and snowing as I approached Cambridge. I realised that I had never driven to Joan's house in the dark and had no real idea of where I was going. I stopped the car and phoned her on my mobile phone. I asked her for directions; she didn't drive so couldn't really help me except to say she was on the north side of town fairly near the Newmarket road (which I already knew). I asked her to put Cedric on, and I asked him for driving directions for the Newmarket road.

'I've no idea,' he responded.

'But you drive there often,' I replied. 'You have just driven there a couple of days ago.'

'Oh, I don't think so – my car's not going you know. I can't tell you how to get here.' And with that he rang off.

I sat fuming in my parked car for a moment or two. This was a man who had prided himself in his navigation skills both in the air and on the ground, and had taught me to read maps for him in the car when we drove together across Europe – 'Don't turn the map around as we change direction – only women do that – always keep north at the top.'

In the end I found Joan's house without too much difficulty. She gave me some sandwiches, showed me where I was to sleep, and asked me to take Cedric out to the local pub so that she could get some peace.

'He can't remember anything, you know. So he keeps repeating the same question over and over again. It drives me mad; please take him away tomorrow.' I said that I would.

It had stopped snowing so I walked him to the nearest pub just five minutes away. I don't think he had ever been in it before – it was rather scruffy and looking distinctly tired after the Christmas festivities. 'I love this pub,' he said on entering. 'Best pub in Sleaford, been using it all my life.'

The next day I bought a new battery for his car which then started immediately, and sent him on his way back to Sleaford.

6

Hawker Hurricane

On 6 April 1941 Germany invaded Yugo-
slavia and Greece, and Cedric took his first
flight in a Hawker Hurricane. This was the
most powerful and the fastest single-engine
machine that Cedric had ever flown.

The Hurricane was the first into production and service of the RAF's single-seat, 8-
gun, Merlin-engined monoplane fighters,
and perhaps the most important. It bore the
brunt of the Luftwaffe onslaught of the
Battle of Britain and, while it didn't acquire
the legendary status of the Spitfire, it was in
many ways a most useful and versatile aircraft. The fuselage, which was partly clad in
fabric, was clearly derived from the Hawker
Fury; the wing was all metal and the main
undercarriage was retractable. It was simple
and relatively cheap to produce – by com-
parison, for example, with the Spitfire. In
test conditions examples reached nearly 400
mph, but the more typical maximum speed

was approaching 350 mph. The Mark I (Mk I) was introduced into RAF service, No. 111 Squadron, in December 1937 and by the outbreak of war 18 more squadrons had been fully equipped with Hurricanes.

Theoretically, and usually in practice, the Hurricane was at a performance disadvantage when engaging the Luftwaffe's contemporary fighter, the Messerschmidt 109 (Me 109). However, its agility, stability as a gun platform and ability to keep flying with substantial damage often enabled it to hold its own, and its firepower proved adequate to knock down other enemy aircraft, particularly in its later 12-machine gun or 4-cannon configurations. As the war progressed its performance disadvantages against progressively improving German fighters increased. It was therefore modified for other missions including bombing and tank destruction for which it was fitted with two 40 mm anti-tank cannon; it was highly successful in both of these roles. Sea Hurricanes adapted for aircraft carrier operation were also developed. Hurricanes were built in Britain and Canada and the total production of all variants was 14,000 of which about 3000 were provided to the Russians.

Cedric's log book records the Hurricane he

flew on 6 April as a Mk III, Serial REX. However, according to histories I have accessed, the Mk III existed only on paper and was never put into production. It is likely that REX was a Mk II A or B fitted with a 1280 horsepower Rolls-Royce Merlin engine. Cedric flew REX twice on 6 April and continued to fly it throughout April interspersed with flights in Proctors, Magisters and Tiger Moths.

It is not clear from his log book from where exactly this flying was taking place. 'Speke' is mentioned as being only a few minutes flying time from where he was based. Speke was Liverpool's civil airport and thus RAF Hooton Park was close – Cedric had been posted there on detachment to No. 13 Squadron from No. 225 Squadron. He may have been flying from both airfields, possibly the Hurricanes were at Speke.

At the end of the first week of May 1941, however, he was with No. 232 Squadron in Ouston, Yorkshire, flying Hurricane Mk Is intensively. He had been selected to command a fighter squadron later in the year and had to be taught and to practise fighter tactics. Hence his log book records exercise such as 'Formation', 'Dog Fight', 'Night Flying' and 'Air Firing'. This training appears to have lasted until the end of August, although his log book is missing exact dates of flights during August.

Other things were also happening to Cedric during the period May to August 1941. He was still making occasional flights in Proctors and Lysanders, and on 10 August he went solo in a twin-engine Wellington bomber after 75 minutes of dual instruction.

The Vickers Wellington was the first of the RAF's 'modern' long-range bombers. Designed by Barnes Wallis (of Dam Busters' Bouncing Bomb fame) it had a unique geodetic (lattice-work) metal structure which could tolerate enormous damage and was relatively cheap to build. In typical bomber configuration the Wellington was powered by two 1500 horsepower, Bristol Hercules radial piston engines, had a maximum speed of 235 mph, could carry 4500 lbs of bombs and was defensively armed with eight turreted machine guns. At the beginning of WW2 it was used for daylight bombing raids over Germany, but losses were so high that it – in common with other RAF bombers – was soon restricted to night-time missions. As more capable heavy bombers joined the RAF, the Wellington was withdrawn from the RAF's Bomber Command operations and moved into other roles, including training and maritime, which were to continue for several years after the end of the war. It was somewhat prophetic that, given later events in his wartime career, Cedric should choose to learn to fly a heavy, twin-engine aircraft at a time that he was clearly being steered into single-seat fighters.

Nonetheless, from 6 May until 23 June he didn't fly at all. I have inferred from recalled conversations with him and other sources that he was with Force 110 in Scotland at this time, possibly training with a group of 'RAF Commandos'. Force 110 was originally established, I understand, as an expeditionary force to create bases in the Azores should Portugal have proved unwilling to give access to Britain. In the event, Portugal stepped up to its obligations as Britain's oldest ally and provided areas for naval and air bases to Britain and America. Force 110 was then focused on other possible invasions, and morphed into a key component of the D-day landings.

I found the following notes about the RAF Commandos on the BBC WW2 Peoples War website, written by Crawley Library on behalf of Leslie Baker.

In 1942, Lord Mountbatten decided that the Royal Air Force should have its own commando units. This met with some opposition from the RAF but eventually in 1942, it was decided to form 15 separate units each comprising approximately 150 personnel. The requirement was basically for skilled technical personnel, mainly from fighter command, who would be willing to train at an appropriate commando school for operating with squadrons who would be supporting invasion forces. The training was done in Scotland at Inveraray and after completion of the commando training these units were dispatched to various theatres of war: the first being the invasion of North Africa. This took place in December 1942, and there were three commando units involved, each of which landed with the invading forces and thereafter serviced aircraft at forward aerodromes and came under the command of the First Army.

Thus it would seem that the RAF Commandos had not been officially formed in May 1941, but they still may have had a genesis at that time as part of Force 110.

Germany invaded Russia (with which it nominally had a non-aggression pact) on 22 June 1941 – Operation 'Barbarossa' – and such was the initial speed of advance that the 880-day siege of Leningrad started just three months later.

Now that I was living back in England, I was able to see Cedric in Sleaford on a regular basis. My business often took me to the then headquarters of the RAF's Logistics Command at Brampton which was less than an hour's drive away from him. Sometimes I would stay the night with him and take him out for a couple of beers and a meal.

On one visit I went to open the fridge which was on a raised dais in the kitchen – the door came away in my hand and fell on the floor, narrowly missing my foot. I noticed that the two door hinges had failed. I called Cedric to show him what had happened – he just propped the door back and told me to be more careful in future. Later I phoned Pat who said that the door had become loose a few days earlier but would remain on its broken hinges if not pulled open too hard. The fridge was old so I told Cedric that he needed a new one – he said he would get one the following day.

On my next visit about a month later there was a large notice on the fridge door, in Cedric's handwriting, 'DOOR LOOSE, OPEN WITH CARE'. He told me that he had ordered a new fridge. A month later the notice was still there on the old fridge; I drove to the local electrical store in his Ford estate car and collected a new one. As so often before, I could not reconcile his lack of action over a blatantly faulty and potentially dangerous fridge with his previous meticulous approach to all things mechanical and electrical: the slightest squeak or rattle from his Aston or Mercedes would precipitate a search until it was located and fixed. How could this be the same man? But of course, it wasn't.

And, unconsciously, I was still in denial. Seeing him just once every few weeks I was never exposed enough to realise just how near he was to being unable to function alone.

At Orchards in the spring of 1996 I answered an evening telephone call from Sleaford. It was from a local farmer I knew quite well, a long-time friend there of both my parents and a regular pub companion to Cedric. He told me that he was speaking on behalf of Cedric's closest Sleaford friends to tell me that they were extremely worried about Cedric. He could no longer reliably find his way around Sleaford. If he drove into town (less than five minutes) he would forget he had taken his car and after having walked home would report it as stolen to the police. At other times he could not find his way home on foot and would be found distressed and lost in the streets. He was repeating himself continually in conversation and asking the same questions as to the whereabouts of his home or car every few minutes, to such an extent that he was being regarded as a nuisance and all but his closest friends had taken to avoiding him. I said that I would take responsibility for Cedric's future.

Orchards was a quite large house; it had a guest suite in a wing separated from the other bedrooms and bathrooms by the kitchen and dining room. Ruth agreed to have Cedric to live with us. We knew that he would not agree to a permanent move – which was what we were planning – but would accept an invitation to spend a couple of weeks with us by the end of which, we hoped, he would regard our home as his. The first thing to do, though, was for me to get Power of Attorney for him.

I drove up to Sleaford. I had no problem with him signing the Power of Attorney with his neighbours as witnesses. I simply explained that if he were to be taken ill I would need to be able to pay bills on his behalf; he saw the logic of this and willingly gave me the mandate I needed. He was also very keen to stay with Ruth and me, so I gave him a written route complete with his destination address and my phone number for the drive in his Ford. We agreed that he would travel the following weekend starting on the Saturday morning so as to avoid business traffic.

Even driving cautiously in his old car, the journey should have taken no longer than five hours and was quite straightforward: from Sleaford straight to the A1, then southwards until joining the M25 London ring road; anti-clockwise around the M25 then onto the M3 southwards until the M27 just north of Southampton; westward on the M27 until it became the A31 and onto Ringwood at the edge of the New Forest; then just another six miles northwards towards Salisbury on the A338 until the turn off for Gorley and direct to Orchards. I had asked Pat to see him off from Sleaford with his suitcase, and to phone me as soon as he had departed. She phoned at 10 a.m. – he was on his way.

The route to the south side of London was well known to him as he and my mother had lived for many years in a flat in Putney while also weekending at the Sleaford bungalow. Even after moving permanently to Sleaford he had often driven down to that area to watch rugby matches at the nearby Twickenham Stadium. His driving skills were still good and I had no doubt that he would arrive safely at Orchards by late afternoon that same day.

Summer days are long in southern England, but by the time it was nearly dark there was still no sign of Cedric. I gradually become more worried and concerned. At 10 p.m. I phoned the police to see if they had any reports of Cedric or his car being in an accident – there was nothing. Ruth suggested that he might have stopped off on the way to see his sister Joyce in North London, or even Joan in Cambridge – both were only a little way off his planned route. I considered phoning them but concluded that they had probably already gone to their beds, and if Cedric were not with one of them it would cause concern to two more members of his family.

At 9 a.m. the following morning, Sunday, the phone rang. It was Cedric to tell me that he was on his way and looking forward to seeing me. I asked him where he was.

'I'm just leaving that small hotel round the corner from the old Putney flat,' he replied. 'I'm on my way now, should be with you by lunch time,' and rang off.

At 11 a.m. there was another phone call. A male voice asked if I were Christopher and said that he was phoning from a roadside café at the junction of the M3 with the M27 just north of Southampton. He explained that he had been hitchhiking from the start of the M3 and had been picked up by Cedric. Cedric had shown him my route instructions but had seemed rather confused. So, on being dropped by Cedric, he had made a note of my phone number and decided to call me. He said that Cedric had got my instructions for the remainder of the route and a good map with him, but nevertheless the hitchhiker was concerned that he might still get lost. I thanked him. My concern for Cedric now turned to anger: What was he doing at the age of eighty-two picking up hitchhikers? Had he no concern for his own safety?

I stumped around the house and my irritation soon subsided. Cedric had been just 30 miles away at around 11 a.m., another hour should see him safely at Orchards.

Noon came and went, then 1p.m. and 2

p.m. Then the phone rang, again a male voice. It was the landlord of a pub in Weymouth which is a seaside town off the A31 some 60 miles past Ringwood. The landlord said Cedric was with him and had just had lunch. I spoke to Cedric. He couldn't explain what he was doing at Weymouth but said that he was about to set out to Gorley again. I told him that he was now just two hours away so he should be with us by 4 p.m.

At 6 p.m. there was still no sign of Cedric. I was now near to tears from my concern and my guilt; how had I ever thought that he would be capable of driving by himself from Sleaford to Orchards? I told Ruth I would walk to the local pub, the Royal Oak, taking our dog with me. Two pints later, she appeared in the bar with Cedric in tow – 'Hello Christopher,' he greeted me. 'I might have guessed that you would be in the pub at this time of day.'

Ruth later explained that shortly after I had gone out she had taken a phone call from our local petrol station, just at the Gorley turn off from the Ringwood–Salisbury road. The attendant there had told her that he had just 'arrested' Cedric as he drove into the petrol station for the third time to ask directions to

Orchards, and was holding him until someone collected him. She had driven the two
miles, told Cedric to follow her, and brought
him straight to the pub.

I drove Cedric's car back to Orchards. I
put it straight into the windowless shed
which passed as a garage and kept the keys.
Cedric never drove again, and within three
weeks he had forgotten that he had ever
owned a car.

7

Supermarine Spitfire

Cedric recorded just three flights in September 1941 – two in a Magister and one in a Tiger Moth. Throughout October, however, he was again involved in the intensive training necessary for him to lead a fighter squadron all of which seems to have taken place from RAF Hooton Park.

On 1 October he took his first flight in a Supermarine Spitfire. This single-seat, all-metal fighter, although an early Mk I production version and in 1941 no longer used as a first-line combat aircraft, would have had performance and characteristics in most flight regimes similar to those of the Hurricane he had recently experienced. It was powered by a Rolls-Royce Merlin II engine developing about 1100 horsepower and mounted eight machine guns in its wings.

Spitfires started entering RAF squadron service just before the beginning of WW2 and remained in production throughout the hostilities. They were adapted for different roles, and performance was continually improved through changes in engines, aerodynamics and structure. At least 24 different marks of land-based Spitfires were produced plus about 11 more navalised versions called the Spiteful, Seafire or Seafang. As development of the Spitfire progressed, Merlin engines were replaced by Rolls-Royce Griffons – of similar configuration but physically quite different – horsepower increased to over 2000, and maximum speed to 450 mph or more. Total production of all varieties of Spitfire was about 22,500 with the most numerous types being the Mk V and Mk IX at around 6000 each. The Spitfire had a reputation approaching the mythic, and Cedric would have regarded this first flight in one as a major career milestone.

His log book shows that his Spitfire training flights during October included formation flying, aerobatics, use of camera gun, stern attacks, and one-on-one dogfights. He was also revising his instrument flying skills with an instructor in Miles Master aircraft. He flew a total of 45 hours during the first week of October.

On 29 October 1941 he took command in

the rank of Squadron Leader of No. 72 Squadron operating out of RAF Gravesend by the Thames Estuary. This squadron was part of No. 11 Group of RAF Fighter Command which had primary responsibility for defending London during daylight from air attacks directed from the east. The squadron had been very active during the Battle of Britain the previous year.

No. 72 Squadron was equipped with the Spitfire Mk V. This was a more capable aircraft than the Mk I previously flown by Cedric. The Merlin 45 engine fitted produced 1470 horsepower and the aircraft had many aerodynamic and other improvements.

Cedric commanded No. 72 Squadron until 8 February 1942. His log book shows that the registration of 'his' aircraft (i.e. the one he usually flew) was 'AD183', but he also occasionally flew a Tiger Moth and a Magister. His log book catalogues his squadron's activities: sweeps over the Channel and French coastal towns, providing air cover to sea convoys, and 'Rhubarbs' (essentially penetrations of enemy airspace, to seek or lure targets).

On 9 November he was not flying AD 183 but another Mk V simply identified as 'H' in his log book. He was leading his squadron on a fighter sweep over Dunkirk when he tangled with a Luftwaffe Focke-Wulf 190 (Fw 190) which he shot down – the first casualty he had inflicted on his enemy. The Fw 190 was a formidable single-seat fighter aircraft powered by a radial piston engine producing about 1600 horsepower. It was typically armed with a mixture of cannon and machine guns. It became the most capable of the Luftwaffe's fighters. It was first used operationally in the summer of 1941 and outclassed the opposing Spitfire Mk V in both speed and agility; it was later itself outclassed by the Spitfire Mk IX.

On 22 November Cedric claimed a share in the destruction of one more Fw 190 and Me 109 while the squadron made a sweep over Le Touquet and Calais; he was flying AD 183. The Me 109 (more correctly Messerschmitt Bf 109) single-engine, single-seat fighter was of similar configuration to the British Hurricane and Spitfire. It was an all-metal monoplane powered by a Daimler Benz, liquid-cooled V12 engine of about 1200 horsepower and, in various guises, was the most numerous of the Luftwaffe's fighters: some 33,000 were produced over nine years of production. The aircraft engaged by Cedric was the 'E variant' (Me

109E). It would have been faster than his Spitfire at altitudes above 20,000 feet, and the fuel injection system of its engine allowed prolonged negative gravity flight without fuel starvation, which the carburetion system of the Spitfire's Merlin engine could not emulate. On the other hand, the Spitfire Mk V was faster below 15,000 feet and could out-turn the German fighter at all altitudes.

The Japanese made their surprise attack on the USA base of Pearl Harbor on 7 December 1941 and the following day both the USA and Britain declared war on Japan. Germany and Italy declared war on the USA on 11 December.

There were to be no more personal air-to-air combat successes for Cedric before he left No. 72 Squadron on 11 February 1942. He flew 103 sorties in his 14 weeks with the squadron.

His last flights as the OC of No. 72 Squadron were on 10 February when he flew a Spitfire to and from the Headquarters of No. 11 Group at RAF Biggin Hill. There he was told that he was to move to RAF Biggin Hill the next day and take up the post of Wing Commander Flying on promotion to that rank. Squadron Leader Brian Kingcombe became the new OC of No. 72 Squadron; he had immense experience as a fighter pilot having damaged or shot down many aircraft during and after the Battle of Britain, skills which he continued to demonstrate for the remainder of the war.

On the night of 11 February three large German warships moved stealthily out of the French Atlantic port of Brest. They were joined by ten destroyers and numerous motor torpedo boats as protective escorts, and the whole naval squadron made a successful dash in broad daylight up the English Channel for ports in Germany, arriving there early on the morning of 13 February. The three large ships were the 32,000-ton battleships *Scharnhorst* and *Gneisenau,* and the heavy cruiser *Prince Eugen.*

The *Scharnhorst* and *Gneisenau* had been in Brest 22 March 1941. They had arrived there for essential repairs following two months of successfully raiding Britain's Atlantic convoys during which they had sunk over 100,000 tons of shipping. The *Scharnhorst* had sunk the aircraft carrier HMS *Glorious* with the loss of 1515 lives as it was evacuating RAF and RAF personnel from Norway after the failure of the Narvik campaign.

The *Prince Eugen* had arrived in Brest on 1 June 1941. She had been part of a German battle group centred on another German battleship, the *Bismarck*. This group had successfully engaged British capital ships from Scapa Flow in the Denmark Straits causing the catastrophic loss of the battleship HMS *Hood* and severely damaging another, the *Prince of Wales*. However, Swordfish torpedo bombers from the aircraft carrier HMS *Victorious* led by Lieutenant Commander Eugene Esmond had subsequently found the *Bismarck* and so disabled it that it was later sunk by other British warships. The *Prince Eugen* had managed to make its escape to Brest.

The Swordfish was a large, single-engine biplane powered by a 750-horsepower Bristol Pegasus radial piston engine. It could be flown off aircraft carriers or airfields, and could be fitted with floats for water-based operations. It carried a crew of either two or three, dependent upon role, including the single pilot. It was slow (maximum speed about 130 mph) and ungainly, and should have been obsolete by the time WW2 started. However, it proved a very effective naval attack weapon when crewed by Fleet Air Arm aircrew of extraordinary bravery who sometimes experienced horrendous casualty rates.

During the months that these three large and dangerous German warships were in Brest they were subjected to repeated attacks by the RAF and waterborne forces. They were badly damaged several times, but each time were successfully repaired by German personnel at Brest. There they were bottled up, devouring German manpower and material resources but contributing nothing to Hitler's war effort. Against the strong advice of his admirals, Hitler ordered that the ships break out of Brest and return to Germany from where they could be better protected while in port.

British naval and air intelligence staffs had anticipated this move, and the RN and RAF were supposedly able to intercept and destroy the ships while at sea. The naval and air planning staffs had even prepared for such an eventuality under the code name Operation Fuller, but the plan was without detail and assumed that the German ships would force the Channel only under the cover of darkness. Furthermore, the operational staffs that were required to take action on launch of Operation Fuller were denied access to the plan.

From the observation of activities around the ships at Brest in the days before 11 February, there were clear indications that a break-out was imminent. Although both the RAF and the RN were aware of what was about to take place, planning and intelligence cooperation between the two services was poor, and the sharing of information within the individual Services, particularly the RAF, was also faulty. No. 11 Group, for example, with its fighter aircraft bases all over the south-east of England, seems to have been almost totally unprepared. Furthermore, the majority of the RAF's Coastal Command twin-engine Bristol Beaufort torpedo bombers – the aircraft with the best chance of sinking the fast-moving warships – were in Scotland awaiting improvement in the weather before they could deploy to bases on the south and east coasts of England.

The German ships should have been engaged by the Beauforts protected by No. 11 Group Spitfires by day, or by night RN Fleet Air Arm Swordfish also protected by No. 11 Group aircraft, and by the shore batteries of Army-manned big guns ranged seawards along the Kent coast at any time. The capital ships of the RN Home Fleet, however, could not have engaged the German flotilla as they were all safely tucked away at Scapa Flow at the northern tip of Scotland. The seeming reluctance of the RN to commit its major battleships was due, perhaps, to the fact that it had lost not only the *Hood* to the *Bismarck* but also that two more of its major battleships – the *Repulse* and the *Prince of Wales* – had been sunk by Japanese air attack off Malaya on 10 December 1941. Churchill wrote this about receiving this news of the Japanese sinkings while in bed:

'In all the war, I never received a more direct shock... As I turned over and twisted in bed the full horror of the news sank in upon me. There were no British or American ships in the Indian Ocean or the Pacific except the American survivors of Pearl Harbor, who were hastening back to California. Over all this vast expanse of waters Japan was supreme (The Allies were left with only three operational capital ships in the Pacific Theatre), *and we everywhere were weak and naked.'*

Only six Swordfish and crews, all from No. 825 Squadron of the Fleet Air Arm, were available to attack the German ships. They were led by Eugene Esmond and detached to RAF Manston on the Kent coast of the Channel to await the passage of the German fleet, supposedly by night.

The departure of the ships from Brest should have been detected by patrolling RAF Coastal Command aircraft, but it wasn't. By the time positive identification had been made by a Spitfire at 10.40 a.m. on 12 February, the ships were already off Le Havre, opposite the Isle of Wight, and about to enter the narrowest part of the Channel. Even when spotted, the British staffs handled the distribution of the news badly – in some quarters it was dismissed as fiction.

The ships sailed on, now joined by a huge Luftwaffe presence from German bases just across the Channel from Kent. The British coastal batteries opened fire too late. British motor torpedo boats from the Kent ports attacked when the German fleet was near Ostend (Belgium coast) but were driven off by German aircraft and motor gun boats.

Those few Beauforts that were available in the South of England had not repositioned to the East Coast, in some cases were incorrectly armed, and crews were inadequately briefed. They were not available to attack the German ships as they entered the narrowest, and potentially most dangerous to them, part of the Channel.

At around mid-day of 12 February the six Swordfish were in the air. They circled above Manston, waiting for an escort of five Spitfire Squadrons from No. 11 Group before setting off to attack the German capital ships. With or without escorts, the Swordfish would have to run the gauntlet of the Luftwaffe and the anti-aircraft screen of the other German warships to press home their attack on the German capital ships. The weather was deteriorating, which was all to the advantage of the German flotilla; to have any chance of success the Swordfish had to get on their way.

Brian Kingcombe with his No. 72 Squadron Spitfires had been at readiness to scramble from Gravesend for most of the morning. When the order finally came to depart for Manston and fly cover for the Swordfish he did not even know that their targets were the German warships. The squadron joined up with the Swordfish and awaited the arrival of the four other Spitfire Squadrons. After a few more minutes, a little after 12.30 p.m., Esmond decided to set off with just the No. 72 Squadron escort, the other protective Spitfires being nowhere to be seen.

The German warships were just 23 miles away. No. 72 Squadron performed as best it could in defending the Swordfish against greatly superior Luftwaffe forces; although the RAF Spitfires succeeded in shooting down at least four Me 109s and Fw 190s they could not prevent the Swordfish being attacked by the German fighters.

The increasingly damaged Swordfish and their wounded crews kept going towards their targets, lining up for their torpedo runs and braving not only the German aircraft but also the motor gunboats and the anti-aircraft armament of the large ships. It was a hopeless endeavour, the Swordfish and their crews were being hit continuously. It was all over by 12.45 p.m: all six Swordfish were shot down, no torpedoes having struck a target. Three of the aircraft with their nine crew simply disappeared without trace. There were only five survivors, three of whom were injured, from the eighteen No. 825 Squadron airmen that had set out. All had displayed outstanding bravery in pressing forward their attacks which, essentially, were suicidal, and all the survivors were decorated – Eugene Esmond was awarded the Victoria Cross posthumously.

The other four Spitfire Squadrons finally joined battle with the Luftwaffe, but only after the Swordfish had all been eliminated. Later in the day the German forces were attacked, courageously and with many casualties, by Beauforts, Wellington and Hudson Bombers of RAF Coastal Command, and RN destroyers, but all without causing significant damage to the capital ships. The *Scharnhorst* and the *Gneisenau* did hit mines laid by the RAF and RN but were not disabled, the flotilla arriving in German waters in the early hours of 13 February.

The dash through the Channel had been a huge tactical success for the Germans and was achieved through the combination of Hitler's will, meticulous planning, and excellent cooperation between the German navy and air force. But it was a strategic failure. The battleships were now effectively bottled up in their German ports; had they attempted to put to sea the Royal Navy would surely have destroyed them with the might of the Home Fleet waiting at Scapa Flow. The threat they had posed to British shipping while based at Brest had been removed.

Gneisenau had to go into dry dock at Kiel for repairs to the damage inflicted by the mines. Two weeks later RAF Bomber Command pounded the ship for three nights running, turning her into a hulk that was later filled with concrete to create a blockship fort off Poland. *Scharnhorst* was attacked at the same time but made her escape unscathed. Six months later, when fully repaired from her encounters with the Channel mines and back at sea, she was cornered off North Cape, Norway, five hundred miles north of the Arctic Circle, by a British flotilla lead by the Battleship HMS *Duke of York* and including three heavy cruisers and other warships. She proved an extremely tough and brave adversary, but eventually she was sunk with the loss of 1940 lives, leaving just 36 survivors to be plucked from the icy seas. The coup de grace included a torpedo from a Norwegian warship which had escaped the German invasion of Norway to join the RN.

Prince Eugen left German waters for Trondheim, Norway on 23 February. She was torpedoed en route by the RN submarine HMS *Trident*. With part of her stern missing she limped into a fjord for shelter, but she never operated at sea again. In 1948 she was sunk during nuclear bomb testing at Bikini Atoll.

The British Government ordered immediate enquiries into what had gone wrong to permit the escape of the German ships from Brest. The war at that time was going badly for the British, and Churchill wanted no hint of incompetence among his service chiefs to be broadcast publicly. The wartime enquiry produced no real answers but a great deal of finger pointing. Despite there being a case for outrage by the RN for the failure of the RAF either to provide adequate support for its Swordfish or to successfully engage the German ships with Coastal Command Beauforts, the primary responsibility for engaging the ships while at sea lay with the capital ships of the Home Fleet – which had remained at Scapa Flow.

Further investigations after the war revealed the full story of distrust, muddle and incompetence, but by this time the principal players had moved on, and some key documentary evidence had conveniently disappeared.

What then of Cedric while all the excitement in the Channel took place? He was at Biggin Hill while Brian Kingcombe took to the skies with No. 72 Squadron, Cedric's squadron of just two days earlier. That the squadron acquitted itself well should reflect not only on Brian's outstanding abilities but also into the work Cedric had put into the squadron over the preceding three months. He did fly on that fateful 12 February: his log book shows that he took a Spitfire MkV up from Biggin Hill for two hours twenty minutes before landing at RAF Eastchurch – another of No. 11 Group's south-east England airfields – the entry reads 'Channel battle – Scharnhorst etc., landed East-church'. Later that day he flew the twenty minutes back to Biggin Hill. His log book gives no other clue as to what he was doing that day or the actual time that he first took off.

On top of the embarrassment to the British Government of the escape of the *Scharnhorst* and *Gneisenau* came the news on 15 February of the fall of Singapore to the Japanese.

Cedric held the post of Wing Commander Flying at RAF Biggin Hill for just two months. He flew a Spitfire occasionally, nearly always the same one 'BH-C', some-times on air tests, other times on offensive sweeps over the Channel. His duties would not have been primarily ones of combat but more probably to seeing that flying stand-ards, procedures and instructions were adhered to. On 13 April 1942 he was posted to what was very much a combat appointment in Malta.

Cedric settled into life with Ruth and me at Orchards. I had to go to my office every day while she conducted her business mainly from home. If she had to go out she always took Cedric with her, either in her car, or on foot walking to the local shop or exercising our dog.

Cedric's car was stowed in the garage and after about three weeks he stopped looking for it. I later arranged for it to be taken away and scrapped. I went back to Sleaford, met with Pat and together we decided which of my parents' possessions to keep. I packed up all the valuables and family pictures and took them with me back to Orchards where I decorated Cedric's rooms with some of them. Heavier items were collected by a removal company and taken to the garage at Orchards. The remainder was given to charities, or scrapped. I then put the bungalow up for sale; it was purchased by a neighbour.

Orchards was 'L' shaped. The older part of the building dated from the 1700s and comprised kitchen, dining room, downstairs bathroom and two living rooms – one with an inglenook fireplace – boiler room and scullery. A staircase led upstairs to two bedrooms, a study and bathroom. The kitchen led through a waist-level swing door to a large breakfast room which formed the ground floor of the newer wing. Another staircase led up from the breakfast room to Cedric's bedroom; at the other end of this bedroom was Cedric's bathroom – this end of the house was to be Cedric's suite and new home.

When Ruth and I had decided to look after Cedric at Orchards we naively imagined a routine in which I could work from 9 to 5 at my office about twenty miles away while she worked from home. When going out she could either take Cedric or leave him at home happy with his own company, and I would take him some evenings to our local pub, the Royal Oak. At weekends he would help me in the garden and come shopping with me to our local market town of Ringwood. We would all live tolerantly in a bucolic contentment; it was not to be.

If either Ruth or I left Cedric alone somewhere in Orchards for more than a minute he would wander through the house calling for us. Privacy, except in our bedroom which was at the opposite end of the house to his, was impossible for us. And even there he would sometimes come banging on the door asking for us, asking where he was, or just bang. He would walk into the bathroom while we were showering, and rattle toilet door handles. Every closed door he regarded as a challenge.

One day I fixed a bolt to the low door between the kitchen and family room, shot it closed, and left Cedric in the family room while I attended to something in the older part of the house; Cedric mastered the bolt and within two minutes was back with us. Another time we bolted the door between the kitchen and dining room while we tried to take time to ourselves in the old part of the house. When I checked on him just twenty minutes later he was well advanced in the removal of a window by unscrewing the hinges with his Swiss Army knife.

The breakfast room was used as a family room and had a television and easy chairs, along with the breakfast table and its chairs. We soon discovered that Cedric was an avid watcher of television news programmes, and that by switching channels we could keep news coming in the evening for an hour and a half. As his short-term memory was

107

already very poor, he couldn't actually remember what he had been watching from one moment to the next, so he would cheerfully watch continuous rehashes of the same news items while Ruth prepared dinner and I talked with her. Those were, however, the only periods of comparative calm; at other times we were bombarded with questions repeated every few minutes no matter how often, how patiently, or how bad-temperedly we answered. Sometimes we felt desperate for time on our own, but it proved elusive.

8

Bristol Beaufighter

In his RAF career up to April 1942 Cedric had flown 1600 hours in sixteen different aircraft types and had experienced combat in Lysander and Spitfire. His war record was good, but far from outstanding, and he had collected none of the fame and glory of the Battle of Britain pilots. With his introduction to the Bristol Beaufighter all that was about to change.

On April 12 1942 Cedric flew for the last time as Wing Commander Flying at RAF Biggin Hill; his log book simply reads 'Spitfire ONH, Aerobatics, 40 minutes'. He was about to go to Malta as Second in Command of Fighters where he would be flying newly delivered Spitfires in defence of this island fortress.

Malta had become critically important to Britain after Italy had entered the war on Germany's side in 1940. It stood in the Mediterranean Sea halfway between Gibraltar and British-held Egypt, astride Britain's trade and military resupply sea route to the Middle East, the Suez Canal, India and the Far East. Without Malta, Britain would have had no way of providing adequate protection to this route and no base from which the Axis forces in North Africa which threatened Egypt could be harried. Yet Malta lay just 100 miles or so from Sicily – the Italian homeland laden with Italian, and increasingly German, aircraft, troops and logistics. Malta came under increasingly heavy air attack from June 1940 and endured siege-like conditions as supply convoys from Gibraltar were decimated by Axis attacks.

From June 1942 the Axis forces in North Africa commanded by Rommel were driving a disorganised British army eastwards and would eventually threaten British-held Egypt itself – the gateway to Arabian oil and India. The Axis siege of Malta conducted by submarines and bombers based in Sicily had by now slightly eased as Allied convoys, much strengthened by the inclusion of American warships and merchantmen, fought their way through the Mediterranean Sea from Gibraltar to deliver aircraft, munitions, fuel, and food. This resupply enabled the island to be better defended by the RAF. It also permitted more effective interference with Rommel's supply routes from Italy and Vichy France, and made it possible to inflict increasing damage to his North Africa forces and to military targets in Italy. Malta's importance to the Allied war effort was, if anything, increasing as it came out of its brave endurance of siege conditions.

However, Malta's resupply was still extremely hazardous and uncertain and the privation of its inhabitants continued; Cedric's weight was to drop from a robust 12 stone (168 lbs) to just 8 (112 lbs) during the eight months he was in Malta. Furthermore, the average lifespan of a wing commander flying combat duties out of Malta was said to be just seven days at the time of his posting there.

In mid-April 1942 Cedric flew to Lisbon in a twin-engine Catalina flying boat and thence onto Malta; this journey is not recorded in his flying log. His Spitfires were transported to Malta aboard the American aircraft carrier Wasp which had loaded 47 Spitfire Mk Vs at Glasgow on 13 April; these aircraft were successfully flown off the carrier and all but one landed in Malta on 20 April. However, the island was being subjected to intensive bombing by the Axis and almost all of these new aircraft were destroyed on the ground immediately after their arrival. By the time Cedric got to Malta he had no aircraft left to command. There was no going back to the UK so he was appointed Air Advisor to the wartime Governor of Malta, Field Marshal Lord Gort; a position he held until August of that year.

Looking at Malta convoy records I discovered that the Wasp and the British carriers Eagle and Argus made six more pilgrimages to Malta before the end of July 1942 carrying a total of 206 Spitfires of which 195 are recorded as arriving on the island. Why Cedric was not given command of some of these aircraft and their crews is not known – perhaps he had already made his mark with Lord Gort.

Those three months of ground tour (his log book doesn't record any flying during the period) must have been extremely frustrating for Cedric: fellow RAF and Commonwealth aircrew were flying intensive combat missions with considerable success, although at great cost in casualties. At the beginning of August, however, he was appointed CO designate of No. 227 Beaufighter Squadron which had recently been equipped with the latest version, the VIc, of the Bristol Aircraft Company's famous and highly effective twin-engine fighter bomber. First, though, he had to refresh his flying skills and learn how to use an aircraft with two engines in combat.

The Beaufighter was developed from a stable of twin-engine Bristol military aircraft which included the Blenheim and Beaufort. The Blenheim was a versatile light bomber powered by two of Bristol's own Mercury or Pegasus radial piston engines producing up to 950 horsepower. It was armed with a ventral gun turret and normally carried a crew of 3.

The Beaufort was developed as a torpedo-bomber from the Blenheim; engine power was increased and the standard crew became four. It was widely used by the RAF as well as Canadian and Australian air forces and proved highly effective, although eventually superseded when Beaufighters were equipped as torpedo-bombers.

The Beaufighter VIc was a powerful, very aggressive-looking aircraft flown by a crew of two: pilot and navigator. Flt. Sgt. Gordon Burnside (soon to be commissioned as a Pilot Officer) was chosen to be Cedric's navigator − they were to become a very effective combination. The VIc was the latest development of earlier marks of Beaufighter. It was powered by two 1670 horsepower Bristol Hercules, sleeve-valve, radial engines which gave a formidable low-level performance, and a challenging swing on takeoff which became more than just challenging if an engine failed immediately after lift-off. It was fitted with four nose cannon and six or eight wing-mounted machine guns. Some aircraft had rearwards-firing machine guns in the wheel fairings to surprise chasing aircraft, while others had provision for 250 lb bombs, rocket projectiles and long-range fuel tanks. It packed a formidable punch which was particularly effective against surface targets. I recalled Cedric saying that when seeking to surprise such targets he flew the aircraft so low that the vortices from its propeller tips left tracks on the sea or desert surface.

Crew losses in the Beaufighter, wherever it operated, were very high as its targets were usually well provided with the means of self-defence. Nevertheless, the aircraft was very popular with its crews, not only because of its effectiveness but also because of its inherent strength that enabled it to take a great deal of punishment and keep flying. If forced down, the armoured cockpit and two huge engines in front provided excellent protection to the crew as the aircraft scythed through immovable objects before coming to rest.

On 4 August he had his first flight in three months: thirty minutes of instruction by Flt. Lt. Edwards in a Beaufighter. Three further solo flights in a Spitfire MK Vc and one in a Hurricane Mk IIb was all he could muster by mid-September at which time he moved to the Suez Canal Zone to continue his training at No. 1 Multi-Engine Training School, El Ballah.

After two hours of instruction at El Ballah on a Bristol Blenheim he was flying it solo. He also found time to air test a Hurricane. On 22 September he progressed to a Beaufighter and passed various flying, navigation and weapons tests. On 10 October, after thirty hours of flying training, he returned to Malta in a Consolidated Liberator bomber and took command of No. 227 Squadron.

The first flight of Cedric and Gordon as a crew was on 13 October, and notable: the log book reads 'Local Test. Hydraulics failed, Crash Landed.' Both appear to have been unhurt as they were flying together again on 15 October. The log shows nine more flights with Gordon up until 4 November; most were air tests or sweeps looking for maritime targets. I knew that this period of commanding No. 227 Squadron was among the most important of Cedric's wartime experiences and his log book was not being much help in my understanding of what went on around Malta in late 1942. As a child I had heard Cedric discussing his wartime experiences but I didn't have enough information. I found a copy of Roy C Nesbit's book *The Armed Rovers* which proved an excellent source for information on Beaufighter operations over the Mediterranean. It also contains much about Cedric himself which Roy could only have gleaned from interviewing him.

Roy Nesbit's book revealed that when Cedric took over command of No. 227 Squadron, which was based at RAF Luqa, it was in bad shape – not in any way because of the leadership of the previous CO, Wing Commander Ross-Shore, but the result of sustained anti-shipping attacks. Several crews had been lost – killed or captured – along with their aircraft. These losses continued in the first month of Cedric's tenure: aircraft crashed through combat damage and others were destroyed on the ground by enemy bombing. By 24 October the squadron was down to just one serviceable aircraft (from a nominal strength of twelve), and on 30 October four aircraft and seven crews – all that could be mustered of the squadron – were detached to Idku (Edku) in Egypt to rest and re-equip. Hence the reference to air tests there in Cedric's log.

Although October 1942 was a bad time for No. 227 Squadron it brought cheering news for Britain. On 23 October the Battle of El Alamein started between Rommel's forces and those of Britain, Australia, New Zealand, South Africa and India – the Eighth Army – all under the command of General Montgomery. Rommel's defeat on 5 November was the most (if not the first) significant land victory for Britain and its allies in the western theatres since the beginning of WW2 and, along with the defeat of a major German army by the Russians at Stalingrad in early 1943, a turning point in the European-centred war. The turning points for the Far Eastern war might be said to have been the earlier victory of the US navy over the Japanese at the 'Battle of the Coral Sea' in May 1942, and the clearance of the Japanese from New Guinea (the Kokoda episode) which was started by a handful of Australians in July and competed by some 45,000 Allied troops in November the same year.

By 6 November Cedric's log shows that he was back at RAF Luqa with his squadron operationally restored.

On 8 November 1942 Operation 'Torch' – the landing by British and American forces on the coasts of Vichy French North-West Africa commenced. To oppose them, and reinforce the rear of Rommel's forces now being driven westwards from El Alamein by the Eighth Army, German troops were immediately moved by air from Sicily to Tunisia. The priority task therefore for No. 227 Squadron and its sister Beaufighter squadron, No. 272, continued to be the interception and destruction of Axis shipping and transport aircraft. On 12 November six aircraft of No. 272 Squadron shot down six Italian Savoia-Marchetta (SM) 75 transport aircraft.

The next day Cedric and No. 227 Squadron were in action; he led four aircraft while Flight Lieutenant Dallas Schmidt (a Canadian pilot who had an exceptionally productive partnership with Beaufighters) led another four. By the end of the 3-hour, 40-minute sortie six enemy aircraft had been shot down and several more damaged.

Cedric claimed two SM81 shot down and two others damaged. The returned gunfire of one of Cedric's opponents disabled the port engine his Beaufighter. Other victims of 227 Squadron that day included a Luftwaffe Dornier Do 24 three-engine monoplane flying boat and Luftwaffe Junkers Ju 52 three-engine transport aircraft. One of the squadron's Beaufighters crashed into the sea on the return journey to Malta with both of the aircrew losing their lives.

On 14 November Cedric and his eight Beaufighters were not so successful in attacking the Axis aerodrome and seaplane base of Bizerta, Tunisia. The squadron was intercepted by Axis Me 109 and Fw 190 fighters against which the Beaufighter was a poor match. Nevertheless one Me 109 was shot down by a squadron member, Pilot Officer Carl Johnson (who later destroyed a Ju 88 – in the same action) and Cedric, with another No. 227 Squadron aircraft destroyed a SM 81. His squadron lost two aircraft and four crew killed during the action – 25 per cent casualties – and didn't reach Bizerta.

On 20 November 227 Squadron had another major day of action. Twelve aircraft (some of which had been fitted with bombs) and crews were available and split into three flights of four which took off at different times and on different missions. According to Roy Nesbitt's book, Cedric shot down one Ca 314 twin-engine Italian fighter bomber (in his log, Cedric identified this aircraft as a SM 79 which was a large Italian tri-motor torpedo bomber) while a second was disposed of by another of his flight. The second flight damaged a small merchant vessel off Sicily. The third flight, led by Dallas Schmidt, also found and damaged other Axis shipping.

Action by Nos. 227 and 272 Squadrons continued at this pace through the remainder of November and December; Cedric even made an 'Offensive Sweep' with Gordon Burnside as crew on Christmas day. Cedric shot down no more aircraft but other members of his squadron, led by him, had more successes against aircraft and inflicted much damage on Italian shipping and land targets. Aircrew casualties continued during this period and the aircraft were often damaged by enemy fire and crashed on landing.

Somewhat typically, as all this action was taking place, Cedric managed to find a Spitfire Vb on 1 December and flew aerobatics in it for thirty minutes.

Cedric was awarded the DFC (Distinguished Flying Cross) on 15 December – the citation reads:

Within two weeks the squadron has destroyed 16 hostile aircraft in combat as well as others on the ground. In attacks on shipping, trains, road columns and fuel dumps much damage and disorganisation were caused. Throughout, Wing Commander Masterman has displayed outstanding leadership.

No average pilot now, all Cedric's careful training at RAF Digby and unbounded enthusiasm and ability for military flying had culminated in these six weeks of action around Malta. He had faithfully repaid the trust and investment that the RAF had placed in him.

On 17 December his log book records a sortie with Gordon Burnside as follows:

Offensive Patrol. Sighted PRU dinghy & pilot. Remained to assist rescue by MSL.

PRU refers to Photo Reconnaissance Unit (most likely a specially prepared, unarmed Spitfire) and MSL to Motor Sea Launch. I have not been able to trace who the PRU pilot was.

Cedric's appointment to No. 227 Squadron ended on 29 December, and the next day he flew his Beaufighter with Gordon Burnside to Heliopolis, near Cairo in Egypt to commence the next phase of his war.

As I wrote this chapter I reflected on the changes in Cedric in the years between his joining the RAF and his time in Malta. In India he had refrained from a bombing operation for fear of killing non-combatants; in Norway he had been incensed by the bombing of Bodø hospital; as a Spitfire pilot he had shot down other fighters with no note in his log book about the fate of their pilots; and in Malta he had had no compunction about destroying troop carrying aircraft and shipping – they were just targets to him. Yet Cedric was a man with great and natural humanitarian instincts. In common with many military pilots, it seems that the human contents of his targets only represented enemy while actually operating or being carried by the targets – once the targets were neutralised they became essentially non-combatants in his mind.

In the two years that he lived at Orchards, Cedric never really grasped where he was or why. Every evening after the 9 p.m. television news he would announce that he was going to bed. We were usually watching the television all together in the breakfast room at the bottom of the stairs; we tried to prevent him getting familiar with the other wing of the house, where Ruth and I lived, in an effort to stop him wandering into our bedroom or bathroom; but the ruse didn't work.

We would say goodnight to one another, then he would peer around the room and ask where his bedroom was. I would point to his stairs, he would say 'Show me, please,' and I would take him up to his room. He would then ask where his bathroom was, I would show him, wish him goodnight again, and leave him to it. Ruth and I would then retreat to our sitting room. Often he would reappear there in his pyjamas, asking again for his bathroom; I would take him back upstairs to show him, with another good-night. This might be repeated three or four times before he finally made it into his bed.

Early the following morning we would find him in the breakfast room waiting for us or, more probably, waiting for he knew not what. But he was always clean, shaved and smartly dressed complete with jacket and tie – he was ready for whatever the day might bring.

Similarly, he could never get to the local shop unaided. Walking there necessitated a right turn out of our short drive, another right turn after 100 yards at the end of our lane, then a 200-yard walk directly to the shop along a country road – but he could never remember which way to turn out of the drive. To begin with I could not rationalise or reconcile this inability of his to find his way. This was a man who had navigated by map, compass and sun while flying in India in the 1930s, who could find his way to targets across the Mediterranean Sea, who had used to be uncomfortable inside a building unless he knew which way north was, and who could tell the time accurately anywhere in the world by regarding the position of the sun, or even of a shadow, Still I didn't get it; I did not, would not or could not realise that he was proceeding, quite happily as it seemed, along a path to mental oblivion.

He was aware that his memory was bad, but he dismissed it as just that – bad memory. He never showed any frustration at being unable to recall events, places or people. Eventually I realised that this lack of concern was not because he couldn't remember the names of the places and people or the events – in his mind they never existed and thus there was nothing to recall.

Over the months following his arrival at Orchards his attitude towards Ruth changed profoundly. To begin with he was well aware that she was my wife. Later, he would think she was the housekeeper (a replacement for Pat who had served him so well at Sleaford). At other times he thought that she was his daughter (he had no daughter – I was the only child) and, on occasion, his wife. But he never regarded me as anybody but his son.

His ability to speak coherently, even persuasively, remained little changed right up to his death. Indeed, many people on first acquaintance found it hard to accept what I would have warned them about his mental deterioration. He could deliver what I came to call 'Generic Speech': if, for example, he was asked what he had eaten for lunch he would reply quickly, positively and believably with, perhaps, 'some roast beef with mashed potatoes and cabbage'; but asked the same question just a minute later would also elicit an equally quick, positive reply but a totally different menu. He spoke only to ask questions, questions that were repeated continuously no matter how often they were responded to. The only effective defence was to respond with a question:

'Now, please, tell me where I am at present.'

'Where do you think you are?'

'I've really no idea.'

'Well, make a guess and I'll tell you when you are right. I'll give you a clue "New Forest".

'Ah! So we are really in the New Forest?'

'Yes.'

'Are we on holiday?'

'No, we live here.'

'Really! We live here! I'd never have guessed, it's all new to me.'

This is typical of what passed for a conversation if I took him to the pub, as I did most evenings during the first few weeks of his stay at Orchards. To keep the initiative with me, I would introduce new conversation topics every few minutes to avoid the repetitive questioning that caused me so much concern and eventual anger.

Cedric always stood his round when taken to a pub. On Saturdays we would go shopping to Ringwood and I would attempt to buy him lunch in the White Star. He would go up to the bar and order two pints of Ringwood Bitter which he paid for while I found a table. He would return to our table with the two beers carried in his perfectly steady hands. After a couple of sips I would pass him a bar meal menu and ask him what he would like to eat. His immediate reaction was that he couldn't afford to eat anything at the published prices. The prices were, in fact very reasonable, and each sandwich or similar cost only about the same as the beer, then about £1.50. If I asked him how much he thought a sandwich should cost he would say 'Oh, about three shillings and sixpence' – a price that might have been charged thirty years earlier in the pre-decimal currency era. Again I could not rationalise what was going on his mind – why should the food seem expensive but the beer reasonable?

Choosing the meal he would like became a pantomime repeated at every pub meal. Not that he was choosy about his food: his wartime experiences had taught him to appreciate food in almost any form and he would eat virtually anything offered. The problem was that whenever he was served a meal he would always complain aloud that it was far too big, that he 'Couldn't possibly eat all of that!' In fact, he could and did, but the initial complaint often caused confusion and worry to the server and embarrassment to me. So I devised a strategy to deal with it. While collecting our second pints of bitter from the bar, I would order something that I knew he would like and something else tasty but smaller for myself – a snack or appetiser. I would arrange for the smaller meal to be served to him, and the larger to me. He would scrutinise the relative size and contents of the two meals. His looked meagre and less appetising (no chips!) compared to mine. So, with the server gone from our table, I would simply swap the plates.

'Here Cedric, they didn't know who was having which meal; this one is yours'.

Thus he got the meal that I had really ordered for him. Mine was a bit small but I put it down to another successful skirmish with my waistline. In any case, he usually didn't finish all of his chips and those un-eaten automatically became mine.

9

Martin Baltimore

By the end of his hectic tour as OC of No. 272 Squadron Cedric was due to be rested from combat duties, so at the beginning of 1943 he was appointed Wing Commander Training at the RAF's East African headquarters in Kenya. He was to be responsible for flying training standards for aircrew located in what was then British East Africa; he was to be based at RAF Eastleigh near Nairobi. He flew from Cairo in the Short Brothers Empire flying boat 'Cambria' – one of approximately thirty examples of this four-engined British civil aircraft operated by British Overseas Airways that was a cousin of the famous Shorts Sunderland maritime patrol flying boat. His new posting was supposed to be a 'rest' for him; however, Eastleigh was home to a variety of Allied aircraft which he found plenty of opportunities to sample.

On 19 January Cedric was flying a De

Havilland Leopard Moth. He appears to have used this aircraft for the next month as his personal transport between several Kenyan airfields: Eastleigh, Nakuru, Nairobi, Nanyuki. He also flew a Percival Gull four times (the Gull was the civil forerunner of the Proctor and essentially identical) as well as an Avro Anson and a De Havilland Rapide.

Both the Anson and Rapide can be broadly described as twin-engine light transport aircraft, but they were very different in configuration. The Rapide (or in military guise the Dominie) first flew in 1934; it was a fabric-covered biplane with fixed undercarriage powered by two 200 horsepower Gypsy Queen engines. It could seat up to eight passengers and had a cruising speed of 130 mph. The RAF used the Dominie as a radio and navigation trainer as well as for general transportation.

The Anson also dated from 1934 and remained in production until 1952 by which time nearly 11,000 examples had been built in the UK and Commonwealth countries. It was a low-wing monoplane, of mainly tubular metal construction, with retractable main undercarriage. It was typically powered by two Armstrong-Siddeley Cheetah radial-piston engines producing about 400 horsepower each to give a cruising speed of around 160 mph. It could carry ten passengers in its light transport role but was also widely used in a variety of airborne training roles.

On 25 February Cedric took a Bristol Blenheim to Nakuru and the following day climbed into the cockpit of a Martin Baltimore complete with crew for his first solo in this American-built aircraft. The Baltimore was built by the Glen-Martin Corporation as a light attack bomber; its configuration and purpose resembled a hybrid of Wellington and Beaufighter, although essentially it was a much improved Blenheim replacement. It was powered by two Wright 1700-horsepower radial-piston engines. It carried a crew of four in very cramped quarters which prevented in-flight movement between crew stations. It was very heavily armed with up to 14 machine guns fitted and an internal bomb-bay.

More Baltimore and Blenheim flights followed in March, mostly annotated in his log book as 'Air Tests', interspersed with Anson flights; he also used a Gloucester Gauntlet (similar to the Gladiator) to check meteorological conditions on several mornings.

Most of the other flights during this period

were between the Kenyan airfields mentioned above, but in mid-April his log book shows that he was preparing for combat again. He improved his night navigation prowess by flying Ansons more often. He flew practice interceptions in another American type – the Grumman Martlet – the British version of the American Navy's Grumman Wildcat. The aircraft, a single-engine monoplane fighter, was designed for aircraft carrier use; it was powered by a Wright Cyclone radial engine of 1200 horsepower and armed with four heavy machine guns. Cedric would have enjoyed flying this fighter on which, it would seem as usual, he had no formal instruction.

At the end of May 1943 he flew a Blenheim Mk IV from Kenya to RAE Shandur in the Canal Zone of Egypt where he became a student at No. 70 Operational Training Unit. There for the next three months he flew Blenheim Mk IVs and Baltimore Mk IIIs around Egypt practising formation flying, bombing and navigation. Pilot Officer Burnside once again is mentioned as a crew member. One of his Blenheim sorties was dedicated to making a film on evasive tactics in the company of Squadron Leader Duke who was flying a Spitfire. After the war

Neville Duke became a test pilot for Hawker Aviation and greatly contributed to the successful development of one of the most outstanding of the early jet fighters – the Hawker Hunter – which at one time held the world air-speed record with him flying.

Italy capitulated to the Allies on 3 September 1943, but fierce resistance would be put up by German forces for many more months as the American and British troops fought their way up the Italian peninsula.

On 2 October 1943 Cedric was appointed OC of 203 Squadron operating Baltimores from an airfield he calls Berka III, near Benghazi, Egypt. For one month he led the squadron on antisubmarine and ship convoy escort over the south-east Mediterranean.

On 1 November he flew his Baltimore for 35 minutes from Heliopolis to somewhere he calls LG 91 (presumably Landing Ground 91) and the same day climbed into a Wellington Mk XIII for a test flight and first solo – the squadron was being re-equipped with Wellingtons in place of the Baltimores. On that flight he took a crew of four including one Flight Lieutenant Fox who, his log book notes, was killed when the same aircraft crashed two days later.

The Wellington Mk XIII was a maritime

patrol aircraft similar to the bomber version he had flown while training on Hurricanes in the summer of 1941 – he had not flown a Wellington since then. This mark of Wellington was modified to carry torpedoes as well as bombs and was fitted with air-to-surface radar.

I had hung several pictures from Cedric's Sleaford home in his bedroom at Orchards: aircraft he had flown, photos of him with City of London friends, and a lovely photo of my mother in her twenties which now graces my study. At the beginning of his time at Orchards I would ask him about the aircraft pictured on his walls and he could easily identify them for what they were: Beaufighter and Spitfire; his friends he identified as just that – friends but without names. A few weeks into his stay I asked about the young lady's portrait – he had no idea; I coached him into answering that she was Cynthia – his wife, my mother – but there was no recognition whatsoever. He could not remember that he had once been married and, even though he knew that I was his son (which he did right up to the time of his death), he could not recognise that he would have been married to have produced a legitimate offspring (in 1942).

After these first few weeks of living with Cedric, Ruth, who was then working part time as a nurse, recognised that Cedric was much more seriously disabled mentally than I would accept; she arranged for him to be interviewed by a doctor specialising in dementia. The doctor's verdict was succinct. 'There is really nothing left inside his head. The problems you are experiencing now will seem minor in a few months or years time.'

He warned of mood swings, irritability, and inappropriate behaviour possibly including violence towards us and others, as Cedric moved further into his eighties. He advised that we must not be afraid to laugh – with him not at him – at humorous things he might do. He recommended that we prepare for the inevitability of having to place him in an institution.

I could not accept that last advice. To me Cedric looked much as he had done for the past fifteen years or so. He remained physically strong. He could still dress, wash and shave himself without reminding. He was polite to strangers, courteous to ladies, had perfect table manners, still read a newspaper and watched the news on television each night. It was just his memory that was at fault, I reasoned. But my ignorant optimism was wrong, and the doctor and Ruth were right.

Gradually Cedric became increasingly difficult for us to handle. He wanted to wear the same clothes each day, swearing that they had only just come from the laundry or dry cleaners and that he had worn something different the day before. We got round that by taking his clothes away from him once he had undressed for bed.

His bathroom suite in Orchards had a bath but no shower, and I could not get him to take a bath by himself – this despite his Sleaford home having only a bath – he simply argued that he had just taken one. I started to supervise his baths but he struggled as I helped him in and out of the tub and I was concerned that I might lose my hold and drop him. So I had a two-person shower with an integral seat built downstairs just off Orchards' laundry room, and when I decided he had to shower I would strip off and go in with him. And to get him to have a shower with me I resorted to blackmail: 'No shower? No pub!'

Ruth's brother John came to visit us from Australia for a few days. I was at work during the day time so she was glad to have him as company to help entertain Cedric. After a couple of days she felt sufficiently confident to leave the two together at Orchards while she went out to work for a few hours. She came back to find Cedric locked in a room by himself with John standing guard outside. There had been a big row between them sparked by Cedric accusing John of being Ruth's lover and ordering him to leave the house. Fearing that he was about to be physically attacked, John managed to get a solid oak door between Cedric and himself.

We now realised that we could never ask anyone to look after Cedric for us either in their own home or ours. Yet I could not expect Ruth to stay at home to look after him – it would have driven her mad, as it would have me. So I acquiesced to her request that he go to a day-care home so that we could both return to some semblance of normality in our home and working lives.

Ruth inspected several care establishments and finally decided on Tern Hall which specialised in long- and short-term care of people with mild to severe dementia. Each morning she took Cedric there and each evening brought him back to Orchards.

We had by now learnt that the only way to prevent Cedric from going into his maddening repetitive questioning mode was to maintain a high level of physical or mental activity initiated by ourselves. So, each evening as soon as I got back from my office I would take Cedric down to the pub for a couple of beers. On our return, Cedric would be placed in front of the television to watch the news while Ruth and I talked and prepared supper. Then we all ate together, cleared away – Cedric joined in quite capably – took the dog for a walk and then looked forward to half-past-nine when on the dot Cedric would announce he was going to bed. The ritual of showing him his bedroom and bathroom several times over then followed and, on a good night, he was sleeping by ten o'clock.

Thus Ruth and I stayed reasonably in control during weekdays, but over Saturday and Sunday we kept Cedric with us. One reason for this, apart from my guilt at putting him out to pasture, was my unhappiness at him being at Tern Hall. At the end of his first week there I instead of Ruth collected him. It was my first visit; I rang the bell, and the alarmed door was opened by a staff member.

Tern Hall was an old Grange and, apart from the addition of several iron fire-escape staircases to its exterior, little altered in appearance from its original design. I stepped into a spacious entrance hall dominated by a large 'Gone with The Wind' wooden staircase. The carer went off to find Cedric, first shutting the entrance door behind me, and I was assailed with the stench of stale urine – the signature, as I would find out, of almost all nursing homes.

A smartly dressed old lady was at the bottom of the stairway, one hand clutching a black hand bag and the other grasping an extension to the banister rail which ran up to the entrance. She walked towards me 'Are you my taxi driver?' she asked. 'I'm waiting for a taxi to take me to my daughter's you know.'

I replied that I wasn't a taxi driver. She turned away, changed hands on the rail and handbag and walked back to the foot of the stairs. She turned back to me, changing hands once more. On reaching me she again asked if I was the taxi driver and I gave her the same reply; she returned back to the stairs, then to me, then to the stairs. My attention was distracted from her by the sight of a man coming into the entrance hall. He had on a short vest and nothing else; he walked once around the room and bumped into Cedric as the carer led him to me. Cedric was pleased to see me, looked the semi-nude man up and down without comment and went through the Hall's entrance door which the carer had opened to let us out saying a cheery 'Good-bye, Cedric, see you on Monday.'

I was staggered by what I had seen but Ruth said that Tern Hall was the best of several she had visited. I felt that I had just peered into Bedlam, though what affected me worse was Cedric's seeming acceptance of the place.

My new job in England was not going well. I had retained all of my responsibilities in Belfast, so I usually spent two days each week there, and the England-based task was huge, having been subjected to poor management prior to purchase of the company. In addition, I was given responsibility for a plant in West Virginia, USA, which I had to visit every six weeks in the face of opposition of Washington-based executives of the Belfast company who wanted responsibility for the facility themselves. This workload coupled with the strain of having Cedric living at our home told on me. I was moving insidiously towards a nervous breakdown. I was well aware of the signs: I was becoming abrasive and impatient at work, sleeping badly and less and less tolerant of Cedric at home. I mostly managed to control myself and mask these symptoms – I just didn't have time to have a breakdown; but I also just didn't have the time to do my job properly and I was asked to leave the company.

I accepted a generous pay-off, which had been written into my contract when I moved from Belfast, and went to talk to the managing director of another company in a similar business to mine. We came to an arrangement by which I would work for him for just four days each week to give me more time with Cedric – with clearly defined, restricted responsibilities and, naturally, rather less salary than I had previously enjoyed. Essentially he was giving me time to heal while permitting me to keep working and retain my pride. The arrangement worked well; I did heal and within a year was on the board of the new company working full time again. My responsibilities within my previous company were split among three newly created positions.

10

Vickers Wellington

On 8 November 1943 Cedric led No. 203 Squadron away from Egypt towards India. He took off from LG 91 with a full crew comprised of Gordon Burnside (now promoted to Flying Officer), Flying Officer Maffey, and Sergeants Lyon, Pearson and McCandlish. He flew 5 hours 35 minutes to Habbaniya near Baghdad, Iraq then, on 9 November 3 hours 35 minutes to Bahrain in the *Gulf.* On 10 November he arrived in Mauripur, Karachi (then India, now Pakistan) after a further 6 hours 35 minutes of flying, and on 15 November he flew on for 3 hours 35 minutes to Santa Cruz where his Squadron was to be based. Santa Cruz is now a suburb of Mumbai (formerly Bombay), India and includes what is now Mumbai International Airport. Cedric would have been pleased to be back in India, a country he loved.

No. 203 Squadron had a maritime patrol

role while based in India. Thus from their arrival in November 1943 until the end of April 1944 Cedric and his squadron scoured the waters to the west of the Indian sub-continent searching for enemy submarines. Cedric's logbook shows that he flew with his crew every second or third day and some of the sorties were very long – over 8 hours – when compared with his previous flying experience. There are no records in his log book of any enemy action, and I think it likely that he found the work rather tedious after his Beaufighter and Spitfire days. Nevertheless, his work and character came to the attention of Lord Louis Mountbatten, then the Supreme Commander for Allied Forces in India fighting the Japanese, and he was transferred to the Joint Planning Staff of Mountbatten's South East Asia Command (SFAC) in Delhi in May 1944, and promoted to the rank of Group Captain.

The invasion of France by the Allies started on 6 June 1944 – 'D Day' – and Paris was liberated from the Germans on 25 August. Although the end of the war in Europe was clearly in sight, with the Russians, Americans, Free French and British with their Empire colleagues pushing back the German forces, there was much hard fighting to go before victory there.

Cedric's task at SEAC was to help with the planning of air support for the Allied push against the Japanese forces in Burma and elsewhere in South East Asia. Thus for the six months following his May 1944 transfer from No. 203 Squadron Cedric did very little piloting. His log book does contain some surprising entries, however.

He records that on 2 October he flew from Colombo (the capital of Ceylon, now Sri Lanka) to Calcutta as co-pilot to Brigadier McConnell in a B25, later that day taking the same aircraft on to Delhi by himself. The B25 'Mitchell' was an American twin-engine medium bomber manufactured by North American Aviation. It was used by many Allied air forces, in every theatre of WW2. In configuration and role it was similar to the Martin Baltimore but had a nose-wheel, tricycle undercarriage in place of the Baltimore's tail wheel. Cedric had never flown a nose-wheeled aircraft before; furthermore, although the B25 could carry a crew of six it seems he flew it alone for 3 hours 20 minutes between Colombo and Delhi.

On 30 December he took up an Argus, the RAF's version of the American F24 Fairchild Provider, single-engine, communications and training aircraft, for an hour and forty minutes of local flying around Delhi.

In January 1945 his log book records him flying two passengers around Southern India in a Percival Proctor.

In February 1945 he moved with Mountbatten's Headquarters into Burma. On the 22nd of that month he had a 40-minute flight to check his proficiency in a six-passenger C-45 Expeditor light transport aircraft. He then piloted Air Marshall Coryton, the commander of the RAF's Third Tactical Air Force operating in India and Burma, around his area of responsibility in this aircraft.

By mid-April he had flown back to India in his Expeditor. On 20 April his log book records a 15-minute flight by himself in an L5. This would have been a Stinson L5 which was widely used as a light liaison and spotting aircraft by the American forces. On 28th of that month he climbed into the cockpit of a Spitfire Mk Vb at Barackpore and spent the next two weeks flying it between various bases in India and Burma.

On 5 May 1945 Cedric flew the Spitfire to Barackpore, near to Calcutta in what is now Bangladesh. There, on 8 May, he joined

General Stratemeyer as co-pilot of his C-47 Dakota, the military version of the famous American DC3 airliner. General Stratemeyer was commander of the US Army's Tenth Air Force which had been integrated with the RAF's Third Tactical Air Force and was operating under Mountbatten's SEAC. Together they flew to Mingladon where Group Captain John Grandy took over as captain of the aircraft – John Grandy later became Chief of the British Air Staff, as Marshall of the Royal Air Force – and they flew onto Akyab in Burma.

Mountbatten had been the Supreme Allied Commander South East Asia since August 1943. Under his leadership, outstanding American and British Generals and Air Marshals had turned a somewhat disparate collection of demoralised soldiers and airmen, who had believed they were making little headway in stemming the tide of Japanese successes in the region, into a lean, effective, cohesive force that eventually outmanoeuvred and outfought their enemy in the air and on the ground. On 6 May 1945 the SEAC forces entered Rangoon, the capital of Burma, which by then had been abandoned by the Japanese.

The war against Germany also ended at

this time, on 8 May 1945. Cedric notes that he celebrated the event in Akyab with Air Commodore, the Earl of Bandon, who was then in command of No. 224 Group which comprised the fighter aircraft elements of the RAF in Burma and Assam.

It seems that the end of the war in Europe and the defeat of Japan in Burma prompted Mountbatten to release Cedric from SEAC. On 21 May Cedric became a passenger on a Liberator aircraft en-route to England. On 25 May 1945 he arrived at RAF Lyneham, a large air-transport base to the west of London. He had been away from England and my mother since April 1942 – three years. He had been away when I was born in June 1942, and when he walked through the door of my mother's house in South London I apparently asked 'Is this the Daddy?' He was 30 years of age.

The clearance of the Japanese from Burma marked a significant victory for the Allies. However, the former were still firmly entrenched in other Pacific Rim war theatres; thus the prospect of perhaps many more years of casualty-laden fighting loomed for the Allies before their eventual defeat of Japan. On 17 July 1945 Mountbatten attended the Potsdam Conference of

Churchill, Truman and Stalin, where he was told of the existence of the atom bomb. The Americans dropped their first atom bomb on Hiroshima on 6 August 1945 and their second on Nagasaki three days later. These horrific attacks lead directly to unconditional surrender by the Japanese on 14 August.

Christmas 1996 came with Cedric still at Tern Hall during week days. Ruth bought half a dozen pairs of socks packed in cardboard tubes for Cedric to give to the male staff and a similar quantity of talcum powder tins for the females. A few days before Christmas I sat Cedric down at the kitchen table with sheets of wrapping paper, scissors, sticky tape and gift cards, and left him to wrap his presents for the Tern Hall staff.

After about twenty minutes I came back into the kitchen to see how he was doing. He had talcum powder in one hand, scissors in the other, and was staring at the wrapping paper – no progress had been made. I asked him what was the matter and he replied that he didn't know what he was supposed to do. I explained again about his gifts for the Tern Hall staff (he had no idea what or who they were) which had to be wrapped in Christmas paper, and I stayed with him to help. Still he made no move. I explained that the first thing to do was to cut the paper to the right size and that I would do that for him. So I cut out rectangular pieces of paper to suit the socks in their tubes, and other similar pieces to suit the tins of talcum.

I put the prepared papers and the gifts in front of him for wrapping. He took a sheet of paper in one hand and a tube of socks in the other, but he had no idea how to bring the two together. I wrapped a pair of socks to show him – 'Just roll the paper around the tube like a Christmas cracker' – but he couldn't follow me. And yet he could dress himself, tie his shoes laces, knot a necktie, and had been driving a car until just a few months earlier. This was a new revelation for me. It seemed that physical things that he had done many times before, perhaps on a daily basis, he was still able to replicate; but he was unable to learn even the most simple of new tasks or, as it proved, old tasks in new surroundings. He could not learn how to turn the Orchards' television on, boil a kettle or find a cereal for breakfast; everything like that would have to be done for him in future. Ruth and I realised that he could never be left alone in the house.

I came back to Orchards from work one evening to find Ruth and Cedric in the kitchen. He greeted me in his usual hearty way and said that he was ready to go out for our evening drink together – this was our established routine by now. Ruth said sharply that she didn't want Cedric to go out to the pub so often and certainly not that evening as he was in disgrace. I asked her what had happened. She described how she had not had to work that day and had decided not to take Cedric to Tern Hall but to keep him company herself. In the morning she had taken him out in the car while she did some local shopping. On the return journey from the shops she had driven past our local pub which Cedric had recognised. He asked that they stop for a drink; she had refused as she had wanted to get home and she didn't support the idea of him going drinking twice in a day. He had then grasped the steering wheel to try and turn the car into the pub car park and kicked her feet away from the pedals; it was only by great luck that the car ended up on a grassy verge rather than hitting something substantial. She was upset and frightened – Cedric was still physically very strong. Later that evening she said that we had to get control of our lives again and that Cedric would have to receive greater and more continuous care than we were able to give – he could no longer live with us full time. I agreed on the understanding that we found him somewhere that was more of a retirement home than a nursing facility, somewhere that did not smell of urine and was not populated by people in the chronic stages of dementia.

We found White Gates on the edge of our local market town of Ringwood and just ten minutes drive away from Orchards. It was a large, Victorian house standing in its own grounds on a private road which also connected via a pedestrian way to the centre of town – a ten-minute walk at most. There were less than a dozen residents all of whom were well dressed. Every resident had a spacious, well-decorated room with its own en suite bathroom. There were pleasant common rooms and the whole facility had the air of a gentlemen's club, except that residents were about equally divided between the sexes. It was run by a resident husband and wife team who were also the owners.

It seemed ideal. Judging by the other

residents, Cedric would be well looked after and comfortable, and he should have been able to make his own way safely to and from the town centre when wishing to shop or visit a pub.

Feedback on his progress by the owners during his first two weeks there was encouraging. He seemed to have settled in well and was finding his way into town every now and again for a pre-lunch pint. I visited him there on a couple of occasions and he seemed happy. However, at the end of his third week Ruth received a phone call from the White Gates owners asking for Cedric to be removed immediately as he had twice punched other residents and had had to be confined to his room. I was away on a business trip so she collected Cedric who, of course, had no recollection of the incidents. She was told that he had become angry when another man, whom he had been pestering with his usual questions, had told him to go away. Cedric had punched this man, fortunately without doing any serious harm, and had repeated the incident with another resident the following day.

So Cedric returned to Orchards, and Ruth and I returned to our previous roles while looking for somewhere more suitable for him to stay. We tried two more local day-care homes: he managed to get expelled from both for abuse of staff and other patients.

11

Avro Anson

Nothing is recorded in Cedric's log book for the month of June 1945; it is probable that he was taking much deserved and needed leave, and getting to know my mother again – and me. In July he took a flight in an Avro York (see below) as an observer of an air-to-air refuelling demonstration. In August he flew a Percival Proctor for 90 minutes

In September he was checked out for piloting the Anson XII and then made several flights, sometimes by himself, around war-torn Europe. He visited Brussels, Paris, The Hague, Copenhagen, and in Germany Buckeberg, Hamburg and Berlin. During this period he was probably attached to some department of the Air Ministry in London. As I read these entries in his log book I wondered what his feelings were as he landed for the first time on German soil on 6 September at Buckeberg. Did he meet any Luftwaffe personnel there? I wished I had asked him these and myriad other questions.

In his new post Cedric had to give up his wartime rank of Group Captain and revert to being a Wing Commander (this rank reduction was common throughout all British Armed Forces as they rapidly shrank to match peacetime requirements). However, his short-service commission was converted to a permanent one, and in April 1946 he was given a place in one of the first RAF postwar Staff College courses, at Bracknell, west of London. During the six months of this course he continued occasionally to fly small training and transport aircraft: Percival Proctor, Airspeed Oxford (a general-purpose training aircraft similar to the Anson), Miles Magister and Dc Havilland Dominie (similar to the Rapide) – whatever he could get his hands on, it would seem.

In September 1946, after his Staff College course, he was posted to RAF Transport Command in the South of England where one of his duties was to help in planning for the new London Airport at Heathrow. He stayed at Transport Command for just nine months and flew only eight times, mostly in Ansons or Oxfords; however, three of these flights typified Cedric's drive to fly anything available.

On 27 November 1946 he had 90 minutes of flight instruction in an Avro York. The York was an inelegant passenger-carrying version of the famous Avro Lancaster heavy bomber. Like the Lancaster, the York was powered by four Rolls-Royce Merlin engines and had a tail wheel; its aerodynamic surfaces, primary structures and systems were all borrowed from the Lancaster. It was the largest and most complicated aircraft that Cedric had flown. The following day he captained it for another 90-minute flight.

On 11 December 1946 he climbed into the cockpit of an ex-Luftwaffe Ju 52 transport aircraft and flew circuits by himself for 25 minutes.

In the summer of 1947 he was posted to Japan as a member of the Allied Occupation Forces. He flew out by civil aircraft, and I and my mother followed some months later in a troop ship – the SS *Lancaster*.

Even before Cedric went to White Gates I had begun to realise that such an open shelter was likely to be inadequate for his eventual needs – the reality of his condition and its inevitable progress was starting to sink into my always denying mind.

One of our favourite walks in the New

Forest took Ruth, me and our dog near to a WW2 sanatorium that had been privately purchased and turned into a substantial residential complex for the aged. It comprised self-contained apartments catering for those capable of independent living with minimal assistance, along with three levels of institutional care: semi-independent retirement living, nursing care for those with mild mental or physical incapacitation, and a fully secure unit for those with severe levels of dementia. The whole facility was called Lindford Park

On receiving Cedric back from White Gates Ruth and I immediately investigated Lindford Park. The location was good – just five miles from our house, on a hill in a picturesque setting – but there was no getting away from its public institutional origins; the complex was two story, brick built, metal windowed and flat roofed – which translated into long corridors with strings of rooms off. Nevertheless, in the retirement and light-nursing areas decor was good, communal rooms spacious and nicely furnished and there was little of that smell of stale urine that I hated so much. We did not inspect the secure premises. We learned that once accepted by Lindford Park residents would never have to leave no matter how much their mental or physical health deteriorated. Fees were affordable and I was ready to accept full-time institutionalisation of Cedric.

I took him to Lindford Park for assessment by its nursing staff. They concluded that he would need to go into the light-nursing facility where he could be given more individual support than was provided in the retirement area. An en suite room was available, and he moved in immediately.

I tried to make his new quarters seem a little like home to him. I took along some of his pictures from Sleaford – aircraft, friends, my mother – books, radio and other mementos of his life; a full wardrobe of clothes and toiletries. There was a small, comfortable bar off the dining room so I provided a generous supply of canned beers for him (some of which were non-alcoholic) and his favourite pewter tankard. I had imagined that I would pop along to see him in the evening and we would go into the bar and have a couple of beers together just like going out to a pub – but it wasn't to work out like that.

He settled in well. The nurses and ancillary staff liked his company and he required little physical attention: he dressed and washed himself in the mornings – always putting on jacket and tie just as he had all of his adult life – and he put himself to bed each evening. The staff coped much better with his incessant questioning than I ever did. Looking back now I realise that they probably had him on some form of sedation to quell the anxiety that led to the questioning – I have no complaint about that. Two beers each evening, one usually non-alcoholic, satisfied him, and he often sat by the nursing station rather than with the other residents who were usually grouped in a nearby television lounge. The home had its own minibus and arranged lots of outings in the local area. Cedric could afford to go on as many as he wanted (the costs were added to the monthly residential bill which I paid from his own bank account into which his pensions were paid). The staff was pleased to take him as travel still interested him and stilled his repetitive, anxiety-based questions; being physically capable, he was also able to help the staff move other less mobile residents in and out of the minibus.

I generally saw him twice each week. I would go to Lindford Park of a weekday evening and usually find him by the side of one of the carers at the nursing station.

'How about a beer, Cedric?'

'What a splendid idea! Where shall we go?'

'Well, let's go to the bar here.'

'Is there a bar here? I never knew that. Just lead the way.'

The carer and I would exchange glances, and I would lead him to the dining-room bar where we would drink a couple of beers each while I answered his usual questions about where he was.

I would then suggest that we went to his room – this was my way of seeing that he had sufficient clothes and toiletries.

'Do I live here?'

'Yes.'

'Really? Please show me where.'

And I would lead him to his room which was not ten yards from the nursing station and had his name on the door with a big picture of a jet airliner placed by one of the carers to show that a pilot lived there.

I would look at his pictures.

'Do you remember flying that aircraft?' I might ask, pointing at a photo of a Beaufighter taking off in Malta.

'No.'

Or, holding a photo portrait of my mother in her thirties, 'Who is that lady?'

'I've no idea.'

'She was your wife.'

'Really! I didn't know I was married.'

'Well, I had to have a mother didn't I?'

'Yes, of course, but who was she?'

And so it would go on; and so I would make my good-byes promising to see him again soon.

Soon was usually Saturday; a trip to Ringwood with beers and lunch in the White Star, or back to Orchards for a few hours. Our route as we drove together to and from Lindford Park took us through pretty, wood-lined lanes. Three or four times on each journey he would ask how many different kinds of trees we could see. I started off by giving a truthful answer:

'Five or six I should think – oak, elm, fir, larch and sycamore perhaps?'

Then, perhaps as I got more irritated I would reply mischievously

'Oh, a hundred and twenty-five I should think.'

'Really! That many?'

Then he would lapse into his newly acquired habit of reciting the number plate of every car we passed. I turned this into a kind of game by encouraging him to try and work out what the three letters of the registration plates might refer to – usually something nonsensical; I quite enjoyed this game and it amused Cedric also.

12

North American Mustang

Cedric's new posting was as Senior Personnel Staff Officer (SPSO) at the RAF base of Iwakuni, which was located across a large bay from the devastated Japanese city of Hiroshima. He, my mother and I lived in a purpose-built RAF bungalow on the base. The Service's elements of Iwakuni comprised British and Australian air force and army personnel, some with accompanying families.

My earliest childhood memories (I was four when I arrived) derive from my time in Japan. There were other children for me to play and go to school with, a swimming pool in which I learned to swim, a military hospital in which I recovered from a mild attack of polio, and two Japanese maids who lived locally to help look after me. I can also remember visiting Hiroshima and being told about the big bomb that had destroyed it. My only memory of the town of Iwakuni itself is of the famous five-arch Kintaikyo Bridge; I made a painting of it in water-colours at the age of five which my mother kept all of her life.

Cedric's job was essentially a non-flying appointment, but in those days all RAF pilots who were physically fit enough were expected to retain flying competence when on ground tours, and Cedric would have looked for opportunities to fly whenever and wherever he could. Thus, between July 1946 and the end of that year Cedric records flying a Taylorcraft Auster ten times on short flights to what were presumably other Occupation Forces' bases around Iwakuni: Eta Jima, Miho and Matsuyama are mentioned in his log. The Auster was a small two- or three-seat observation and light communications aircraft of American origin but licence built in Britain in large quantities.

On 9 September 1946 he made a 40-minute solo flight in a North American Harvard. This capable, two-seater, American-designed, single-engine advanced trainer had become the aircraft of choice of several air forces for advanced flying training, and many RAF bases had them on strength for non-operational pilots to maintain their flying proficiency. It had a retractable under-carriage and was usually powered by a Pratt & Whitney rotary piston engine of about 600 horsepower. The Harvard was the British and Canadian designation for the North American AT-6 Texan which was built in America in large quantities. Cedric did not fly in a military aircraft at all in 1947. In February and April 1948 he made three flights as co-pilot in a Dakota, and two more Auster trips. But he had his eye on a far more interesting aircraft.

On the 4 May 1948 Flight Lieutenant Harvey flew with Cedric in a Harvard on what Cedric's logbook records as a 40 minute 'checkout'. This wasn't a check of Harvey's prowess in a Harvard but rather of Cedric's readiness to fly fighter aircraft once again. He clearly passed, and later the same day he took up a North American P51 Mustang for the first time. The Mustang probably represents the paradigm for WW2 single-piston-engine fighters. Once the original American Alison engine had been replaced with the Rolls-Royce Merlin, often licence built by Packard in America, it could hold its own against any-thing then flying – including, on odd occa-sions, the Me 262 twin-engined jet fighter of the Luftwaffe.

Cedric would have loved to fly this aeroplane, which had a better performance than any other aircraft he had flown – and fly it he did on many occasions over the succeeding four months. Iwakuni was the home base for three Royal Australian Air Force (RAAF) Mustang squadrons – some, at least, of these aircraft would have been manufactured in Australia. The squadrons arrived from their original Occupation Forces Japan base of Bofu in 1948, which probably explains why Cedric had to wait nearly a year at Iwakuni before getting to fly one.

Quite how regularly flying a Mustang squared with his ground duties as SPSO I cannot imagine: it may be, however, that he was moved locally from SPSO to flying duties. In the late 1960s I was serving at RAF Cranwell in Lincolnshire (not far from where Cedric had first learned to fly at RAF Digby). The Commanding Officer of RAF Cranwell then was Group Captain Pendred who told me that he had flown Mustangs in Japan under the command of Cedric, and remarked what an exceptional pilot and leader he had been.

Towards the end of 1948 Cedric was posted back to the UK. He flew back and, as on the outward trip, my mother and I followed in a troop ship, the SS *Strathnaver.*

Cedric's months at Lindford Park passed tranquilly for Ruth and me. He was visited regularly by me, and sometimes by Ruth alone; she formed a quite close relationship with the nurse most responsible for his care. He remained clean, tidy and healthy, and seemed happy with his surroundings; I was satisfied that he was being well looked after and cared for, and I accepted that he was now institutionalised.

My elder daughter, Amanda, and her husband came to England from Montreal to spend Christmas 1998 at Orchards. They had not seen Cedric for several years and immediately noticed the deterioration in his mind, but were pleased to see him well settled. We all spent a lot of time with him both at Lindford Park and taking him out for walks and pub visits.

Lindford Park put on a Christmas Day lunch for residents and families so we booked a table for the five of us. We arrived there an hour or so before lunch laden with beer, champagne, nibbles, Christmas crackers and small gifts for Cedric. As we sat in the bar drinking with him, all wearing paper hats from the crackers we had pulled, a member of the staff entered dressed as Father Christmas. He 'Ho-Ho-Hoed' Cedric, gave him a wrapped gift, wished him a Merry Christmas, and departed to repeat the process with other residents.

'Who the hell was that?' was Cedric's only comment, as he unwrapped the beer mug the staff had clubbed together to buy him.

13

De Havilland Tiger Moth

Cedric returned to England in late 1948. He was posted to the Air Ministry in London and lived with me and my mother in South London. His work would have kept him very busy as he arrived to join in the planning and organisation of what was probably the greatest humanitarian event in aviation history – the 'Berlin Airlift'.

At the end of WW2 the defeated Germany was divided into two along a roughly North South axis: East Germany firmly under a very harsh occupation by the Soviet Union, and West Germany occupied principally by American, British and French forces, but also Dutch, Belgian and others. This seemingly neat arrangement had, however, a major complication. Berlin, the traditional capital city of Germany, was well inside East Germany and was split into four sectors of foreign control: the American, British and French Sectors comprising about three fifths of the total area, and the Soviet Sector being the remainder. There were supposedly sacrosanct rail, road and air corridors from West Germany into Berlin. The four victorious allies formed a provisional government which was to control and rebuild Berlin. However, acute tensions between the Soviets and the other three 'Western Powers' soon emerged from unbridgeable differences in ideologies.

Stalin wanted the Western Powers out of Berlin so, through the early part of 1948, the Russians put increasing pressure on them and on the two million Berliners. Events climaxed in late June 1948, by which time the Russians had blocked all land and rail access to Berlin and disrupted other methods of communication.

The Western Powers examined several different options for keeping Berlin supplied with the essentials for living, but the only choice that would hopefully not precipitate WW3 was to supply by air. The freedom for the Western Powers to use three twenty-mile-wide air corridors into Berlin from their bases in West Germany was written clearly into a treaty with the Soviets; it was believed, more or less correctly as it turned out, that the Soviets would not violate this agreement. Two airfields were initially available in Berlin: Templehof in the American Sector and Gatow in the British. When these two proved inadequate a third was built in just three months in late 1948 – Tegal, which years later became Berlin's premier airport.

It was initially calculated that 1,500 tons of supplies would be needed each day to keep the population and the occupation forces sustained. The transport aircraft then available to the Western Powers had usable payloads of between three and ten tons. An average load of, say, five tons would necessitate 300 flights each day from West Germany, or one every five minutes day and night. It was a formidable undertaking and it did not go smoothly for several months. Furthermore, the 1,500 tons did not include fuel - oil and coal – to provide heat for the population during the typically harsh central European winter, to generate electricity, which had been cut off by the Soviets, and to produce energy for the gradual rebuilding of West Berlin's industrial base. Recalculation showed that in the coming winter about 3,500 tons would have to be moved each day by approximately 1,000 flights.

Larger American transport aircraft were drafted to the task and the British threw in almost every thing they had: Yorks, Sunderland flying boats (using Berlin's Havel Lake), Lancasters and Hastings. Superb airmanship and meticulous planning prevailed against bad weather and continual Soviet harassment of aircraft using the air corridors (no aircraft were ever shot down, however). Operations continued 24 hours per day and aircraft arrivals were spaced just two minutes apart – a missed approach to any Berlin airfield meant a direct return to the West without landing. The German population participated in the unloading of aircraft, and ex-Luftwaffe mechanics were used for aircraft maintenance. Eventually, aircraft were being unloaded and sent back to West Germany to reload in 25 minutes or less.

In early 1949 daily tonnage transported was exceeding minimum requirements and conditions for the besieged Berliners gradually improved. By April 1949 daily movements were regularly reaching nearly 9,000 tons, and on one day – intended as a showpiece for the benefit of the Soviets – nearly 13,000 tons was airlifted in 1,383 flights.

By the spring of 1949 the Russians realised that their blockade tactics were not going to force the Western Powers to leave Berlin, and on 12 May they lifted the blockade. However the airlift was by then running so efficiently that Berlin continued to be supplied by air for another four months; the Berlin Airlift officially ended on 30 September 1949. More than 2.3 million tons had been flown in – over half a million tons by the RAF and almost all of the remainder by the Americans. Over 277,000 flights had been made and inevitably there had been casualties from accidents – 101 personnel died. But the Berlin population had been saved without a shot being fired and they now regarded the Western Powers as allies rather than occupiers.

Although I have no knowledge of Cedric's exact duties during the Berlin Airlift, I know that he was very proud to have been involved.

Cedric's appointment at the Air Ministry lasted until early 1950. It was a non-flying post, and to remain eligible for another flying job he had to keep up his flying skills; this he seems to have done during August 1949 when he went to RAF Finningley, South Yorkshire for two weeks. There, under the tutelage of Flight Lieutenant Dudding, he refreshed himself on the Harvard and Spitfire during thirteen flights which included much instrument flying work.

Sometime in the first two months of 1950 he was again posted abroad, this time to an intelligence post in Singapore. This was again a ground tour in the rank of Wing Commander, but was no peacetime sinecure as the British administration in Malaya was facing a major Communist insurgency and the three-year Korean War would start in the middle of the year.

My mother and I followed Cedric to Singapore a little later. For this long journey we flew in a British Overseas Airways Corporation Lockheed Super Constellation; we travelled first class and the journey took three days with night stops in Cairo and Karachi – an exciting first flight for me. On Singapore Island we lived in a spacious bungalow on an estate off the Bukit Tima Road and outside (then, at least) the main area of Singapore City. We had a family of Chinese servants living at one end of the house, and for my education I was sent to a Catholic, multi-racial, convent day-school which took a few boys up to the age of ten. I had a wonderful life in Singapore.

I have no real idea of what Cedric was doing in Singapore. I know it was defence intelligence related, because one room of our bungalow was blacked out so that my mother, who had trained as a commercial artist, could trace maps by hand and Cedric often (or so it seemed to me) had to go 'up country' meaning into mainland Malaya. He also visited Thailand, Burma and India and at times he kept a Browning automatic pistol on his person. During the anti-European 'Maria Hertog' riots of 1950 he had to leave my mother and me alone in the bungalow while he went to the residence of the British High Commissioner.

Although Cedric's new post did not directly involve him in any military flying, he nevertheless managed to fly more during his two years in Singapore than at any other time in his life. He joined the Royal Singapore Flying Club which had premises on Kalang airfield – then Singapore's international airport. With his extensive, hands-on, experience of flying training he soon became the club's vice president and chief flying instructor. The club had a fleet of ex-RAF Tiger Moths together with one or two Cessnas (light American civil aircraft) and Austers. He made his first two flights there on 11 March 1950 in a Tiger Moth registered as VR-SDA. The next day he flew fourteen instructional flights with ten different students.

He continued instructing at the club, although at somewhat reduced frequency, until the end of October 1951. In that period he flew 402 mainly instructional sorties in Tiger Moths (or occasionally a Cessna or Auster) with many different students. I recognised the names of some of those recorded in his flying log, particularly those of whom had children of similar age to me – Trefusis and Trepass. Sometimes he took me and my mother up – I sat on her lap. This, to me, extraordinary pace of civilian flying was in addition to other flights in a plethora of military aircraft of which it seems he had free choice at the RAF Singapore bases of Seletar, Changi and Tengah.

The first of his flights in Singapore-based RAF aircraft was on 3 January 1951 when he was taken up by Flight Lieutenant Collins in a Gloucester Meteor Mk VII (or T7') two-seat, twin-jet aircraft. The Meteor was the first of the RAF's jet fighters and was the only Allied gas-turbine-powered aircraft to see service in WW2. Later versions briefly held the world airspeed record at over 600 mph.

This first flight by Cedric in a jet aircraft lasted forty minutes and was described in his log book as 'Aerobatics and Familiarisation'. A second flight in the same aircraft but with a different instructor took place on 24 February, and another with Collins again on 3 March. These three flights comprised Cedric's conversion from 400 mph piston engine aircraft to 600 mph jets.

On 31 March he took up, by himself, a Hawker Tempest. This large and extremely powerful (2500 horsepower typically) single-piston engine fighter would have been a huge contrast to the petite Tiger Moths he had been so regularly flying. The Hawker Tempest was manufactured in several different marks which were powered by various Rolls-Royce, Napier or Bristol engines. Cedric's log book does not say which mark he was flying but it was probably a Tempest II with a Bristol Centaurus radial piston engine. The aircraft would have been capable of over 450 mph in level flight and during the latter stages of WW2 had proved fast and agile enough at low to medium altitudes to tangle successfully with the Me 262.

On 7 April he helped himself to a Spitfire Mk 22 (Spitfire nomenclature had switched from Roman to Numeric numerals after the Mk XX). This late model Spitfire was a very different aircraft from the earlier marks with which Cedric was familiar: larger, heavier, and faster (450+ mph) with a 2350 horse-power, Rolls-Royce Griffon engine driving a five-bladed propeller, and armed with four cannon.

Perhaps by this time flying bureaucracy at the RAF airfields had caught up with him, because on 20 April he made three flights in a Harvard under instruction to brush up his instrument-flying procedures. This training seems to have rewarded Cedric because on 1 May he took up a single-seat, De Havilland Vampire Mk V (or FB 5), single-jet-engine fighter bomber; his first solo flight in a jet aircraft. The Vampire was developed during WW2 but first examples arrived too late to see operational service.

On 19 June he again flew a Harvard to practise instrument flying with Flight Lieutenant Sutton, but for this flight he records himself as captain of the aircraft so perhaps he was checking out Sutton.

In early July 1951 his log book records three flights, with Flight Lieutenant Collins again, in a De Havilland Mosquito. This was another first for Cedric. The Mosquito was perhaps the most versatile aircraft used by the RAF during WW2. Developed initially by De Havilland as a private-venture light bomber (i.e. without government funding or a specific RAF requirement), it was of mainly wooden construction and powered by two Rolls-Royce Merlin engines. Although its basic configuration was similar to that of his beloved Beaufighter, he may have found the Mosquito in many ways a more pleasant and aerodynamically capable aircraft to fly.

At the end of July Cedric was back in the cockpits of Harvards flying more dual-instrument and night-flying practice, which culminated again in a solo flight in a Vampire on 3 August.

As the third quarter of 1951 drew on he continued to combine instruction on the flying club Tiger Moths with occasional solo flights in Vampires and dual flights in Meteors.

Cedric's last recorded flight with the Royal Singapore Flying Club is dated 25 October 1951, but he stayed in Singapore until April the following year; I wasn't able to ascertain why he stopped flying the club's aircraft for these last six months of his posting. He did take himself off to India on a motor bike for two months or more, and perhaps this trip occurred then because his log book shows no flight from 25 October until 20 December when he co-piloted a

Dakota around mainland Malaya.

In February 1952 Cedric's log book records two flights by him as co-pilot of a Sunderland. The Shorts Sunderland was a large, four-piston-engine flying boat used on maritime patrol and anti-submarine duties. It was possibly the largest aircraft ever flown by Cedric, and operating an aircraft from water would have been a novel and interesting experience for him.

As the April 1952 time approached for him to return to the UK he continued to fly a mixture of military aircraft: Harvards, Meteors and Vampires. His last flight in Singapore was solo in a Spitfire Mk XIX; this photo-reconnaissance aircraft powered by a Rolls-Royce Griffon engine, was un-armed, pressurised and probably the fastest and highest flying Spitfire that he had flown – he would have thought this flight a thoroughly fitting end to his time in the Far East. Coincidently, it was a Mk XIX that flew the last operational Spitfire sortie with the RAF in 1954.

We travelled back to Europe as a family on an Italian passenger ship – the *Roma* of the Flotta Laura line. Cedric had arranged for our car, a British Hillman Minx, to accompany us. We landed in Naples where the car was unloaded and we took a leisurely six-week road trip back to England through Italy, France and the Alpine passes in between, with stops in many of the major cities en route. Cedric taught me to read a road map for this trip, so I took pride in helping him to navigate from a 'Europa Touring' road atlas.

Early in 1999 I received a phone call from Cedric's Lindford Park home inviting me to a review of Cedric's health. I went there with Ruth. We met with the director of the establishment and the nurse in charge of Cedric's facility. They told us that Cedric's mental state had deteriorated to the point where he needed more support than he was currently receiving; he would have to go into the Lindford Park secure facility for the seriously mentally and physically disabled. This was an unexpected blow. I had not noticed any serious deterioration but I reasoned that by only seeing him for quite short periods a couple of times each week I was sheltering myself from reality.

I asked to see inside the secure facility. We were taken through a series of locked doors into what I took to be a scene from Dante's *Inferno*. The smell of humanity stunned me as my senses took in a scene of old people, apparently dressed in nightclothes, waving, shouting, sitting like zombies, being fed, being cleaned, being fought. I turned round and left, gagging or crying – I couldn't distinguish. I told Ruth and the staff that there was no way that Cedric was going into that cauldron and asked for him to stay where he was for a further two weeks while I found him some other place to live.

Ruth's medical contacts in Salisbury recommended a private nursing home – Glenside Manor – about five miles out of the city; it was expensive but had an excellent reputation. We went to inspect it.

Glenside Manor looked every inch the traditional English manor house. It was situated in its own large grounds on a small hill overlooking the River Wiley. There was a large, new, architecturally sympathetic wing attached to the old building. After preliminary discussions with the manager in her office, we learned that there was a room available that could suit Cedric; he could move in immediately, subject to an assessment of his condition and our approval of the facilities in the old part of the building.

The old building had been substantially altered internally from its original configuration. It now had en suite bedrooms in short, spacious corridors leading from a central area where the patients spent their waking hours. This central area comprised a dining room leading off to several rooms of various sizes separated by low walls; some of these rooms were in light and airy conservatories flowing into the attractive gardens. The layout permitted quiet areas for some residents, TV-watching stations for others, and semi-private places for visits. The whole was cleverly configured such that all areas were clearly visible from a central nursing station aided by close-circuit TV to monitor any obscured areas such as corridors and entrance doors. There was an abundance of neatly uniformed staff, and all the patients that we saw were cleanly dressed – not in night clothes – and most were engaged in some form of activity or quietly asleep; none looked as if they were suffering hours of abandonment. A large, well-equipped kitchen was immediately adjacent to the dining room so that food could be freshly prepared for each meal and served without the typical institutional requirement for reheating. We subsequently learned that the new wing was a specialist facility catering for the chronically physically disabled of all ages.

We were impressed by the facilities and the staff so, although the fees were very high, we asked that Cedric be assessed for residence there. He was accepted as suitable and moved by the Glenside staff from Lindford Park within the week.

Over the months that Cedric was there I continued my pattern of visits but gradually he became less keen to go out in my car, or even leave the confines of the home. I also started to notice deterioration in his physical condition. There was a very pleasant pub by the entrance drive to Glenside Manor just 100 yards walk down a sloping drive. I walked Cedric down there a few times but his gait was becoming stiffer and stiffer and he complained of breathlessness, so we confined our walks to a few minutes around the gardens surrounding the home.

His personal appearance also started to deteriorate a little. Sometimes I would find him with a neck tie around his waist instead of his usual belt. I would find the belt in one of the drawers of his room and replace it around his pants. On one occasion I found him without his watch – a very valuable Girard Perregaux – he hadn't noticed it was missing. I managed to retrieve it from the home's lost & found box and kept it in my possession. I bought Cedric a similar-looking, cheap electronic watch which he insisted on trying to wind and thus it never indicated the correct time.

He seemed happy enough in his new surroundings. I generally found him by the Nurses' Station trying to engage the staff in conversation – they made time for him as best they could while dealing with more demanding residents. He also sometimes chatted with the other residents, though what about I have no idea. I took to having a meal with him in the home rather than taking him out. He thought he was taking me out and always tried to pay the staff when we had finished eating. The food was good, the surroundings clean, and the staff attentive; I was happy for him to be there.

14

De Havilland Chipmunk

Cedric's new post was again London based at the Air Ministry, and to do with air transport. I remember him telling someone in later years that it had been his intention in this post to fly every type of transport aircraft in the RAF's inventory, even though his was essentially a ground appointment. I think one of his main tasks was to help define the next generation of large transport aircraft: he certainly had something to do with the introduction into service of the Bristol Britannia four-turbo-propeller engine, passenger aircraft and the Blackburn Beverly four-piston-engine, heavy-lift aircraft.

No matter that the post did not involve operational flying, he was soon piloting aircraft from RAF Hendon airfield on the northern edge of London. In July and August 1952 he was taking solo trips from there in Percival Proctors and Avro Ansons. On 29 August he joined Wing Commander Sellick, an old friend, as co-pilot of a Handley Page Hastings on a trip from RAF Lyneham (a large transport airfield to the west of London) to Gibraltar and return. The Hastings was a large, four-piston-engine passenger transport of tail-wheel configuration which made it look ungainly on the ground.

Cedric did not fly again until January 1953 where he underwent formal training in piloting the Hastings. He also had a familiarisation trip in a Vickers Valetta, the military version of the civil Vickers Viking twin-piston-engine transport aircraft which perhaps is best described as a postwar British attempt to emulate the prewar American DC3 Dakota – the configurations of the two aircraft were very similar. The RAF replaced its Dakotas with Valettas.

Cedric's eyes were not entirely on transport aircraft at this time for in mid-March 1953 he spent three days refresher flying of Meteors.

On 28 May Cedric was again in the co-pilot's seat of a Hastings at RAF Lyneham. With Flight Lieutenant Hall as the aircraft's captain, he flew to Africa before returning to Lyneham. The route as recorded in Cedric's logbook was Lyneham – Buckeburg (Germany) – Wunstorf (Germany) – Istres

(France) – Luqa (Malta) – El Adem (Libya) – Fayid (Egypt) – Khartoum (Sudan) – Juba (Sudan) – Entebbe (Uganda) – Tabora (now Tanzania) – Lusaka (now Zambia) – New Salisbury (now Harare, Zimbabwe) – Gatooma (now Zimbabwe) – New Salisbury – Lusaka – Entebbe – Khartoum – Fayid – Hal Far (Malta) – Lyneham. The trip lasted three weeks and the longest leg was the last five hours from Malta to Lyneham.

On 17 July 1953 Cedric was checked out to fly a De Havilland Chipmunk at RAF Hendon... The Chipmunk was the RAF's replacement for the De Havilland Tiger Moth in the basic training role. It was designed and manufactured in Canada as a tandem-seat, training monoplane powered by a 145 horsepower, in-line De Havilland Gypsy Major 8 engine – a direct descendant of the Tiger Moth's power plant. Capable of more advanced aerobatics than the Tiger Moth, Cedric would have found it fun to fly, and for the next six weeks he used one to visit several other RAF UK airfields in one: Horsham St Faith, Raynham, Southend, Cardiff, Fairfield Common and Lyneham.

In August it was time for Cedric to renew his instrument rating – his 'Green Ticket'. He did this in an Airspeed Oxford; his log book records that after fourteen flights he successfully passed his Instrument Rating Test. Although his log book does not record where these flights took place I believe they were from RAF Lossiemouth near the town of Nairn in Scotland, and were combined with a summer holiday there with my mother and me. There were to be only seven more flights in an Oxford and three in a Percival Prentice (a two-seat trainer contemporary of the Chipmunk, more powerful but less successful) during the remainder of 1953.

On 13 April 1954 he was back in the cockpit of an Anson. After a 25-minute check flight that day (he hadn't flown an Anson for nearly two years), he made a further seven flights over three weeks between Hendon and other RAF UK airfields: Wyton, Aldergrove (Northern Ireland) and Dishforth.

On 10 May he was instructed for 75 minutes on a new aircraft, the Percival Pembroke; he then took it up for a further three hours by himself for, as recorded in his log, 'handling practice'. The Pembroke was a high-wing, twin-engine, metal monoplane capable of carrying eight passengers and two crew. It was the military version of the Percival Prince civil aircraft. One of its principal roles was to provide short-range

VIP transport, and some became the semi-private mounts of very senior RAF officers.

Cedric's conversion onto the Pembroke appears to have been more formal, rigorous and lengthier than any for any previous aircraft. This would have been not only because of tighter peacetime supervision over flying training but also because he was about to make a major long-distance flight in this essentially medium-range communications aircraft.

On 25 May, with Master Navigator Pontet as crew but no copilot, Cedric set off in Pembroke Number 709 to Singapore and arrived there on 6 June. The route taken was Istres (France) – Elaouna (Tunisia) – Idris (Libya) – El Adem (Libya) – Amman (Jordan) – Habbanyia (Iraq) – Bahrain (Gulf States) Sharjah (Gulf States) – Masirah (Gulf States) – Mauripur (Karachi, Pakistan) – Palam (New Delhi, India) – Dum Dum (Calcutta, India) – Mingaladon (Burma) – Don Maung (Bangkok, Thailand) – Butterworth (Malaya) – Changi (Singapore). The flight seemingly was without incident except for having to return to Don Maung en route to Butterworth to sit out monsoon activity. Total flying time was 57 hours and the longest leg was five hours between El Adam and Amman.

Back in England in July 1954, there were more Anson flights throughout the remainder of the year interspersed with conversion in August onto the RAF's new advanced trainer, the Bolton Paul Balliol. This aircraft was an all metal monoplane powered by a Rolls-Royce Merlin engine.

In October Cedric took an Anson from Hendon to RAF bases in Germany – Gatow, Buckeburg, and Wildenrath – followed by another trip around southern UK airfields

He next flew in February 1955 – again an Anson around UK RAF airfields. Then in March he took odd flights in Chipmunks, Meteors, and Valettas, and on 21 April two flights in a Mosquito under dual instruction.

By now, Cedric had passed his fortieth birthday (25 September 1954) and had remained in the same rank of Wing Commander for the ten years since being demoted at the end of WW2. He would have been looking for promotion and a new posting, preferably as Commanding Officer of an operational RAF flying station. All the same, he would not have to stay in the RAF to earn a living as, through my mother's father, he had an open door into the financial world of the City of London. He would soon have to make choices about the future direction of his life.

He would have had discussions with the Air Secretary's branch of the RAF which was responsible for the promotion and appointments of all RAF officers. He was told (around April 1955 I infer from my own RAF experience) that he was being offered the post of British Air Attaché to the former Czechoslovakian Republic. The post would come with promotion to the substantive rank of Group Captain and he would be living behind the Iron Curtain in Prague. He may have been told that there was unlikely to be further promotion for him and he should consider retiring from the RAF at the end of the appointment. Cedric accepted the post knowing, I think, that it was to be his last in his RAF career.

The months before taking up his new appointment would have been extremely busy for Cedric. He would have been subjected to intensive military intelligence briefings together with formal instruction to improve his spoken French which was still then the common language of diplomacy. He would have known that he would soon lose any reason to continue keeping in flying practice so, on 26 May 1955, he took a Chipmunk for a short flight from Hendon to RAF Benson in Oxfordshire. There he flew twice in a Meteor with Flight Lieutenant Hamley, and then he took the Chipmunk back to Hendon – and that was it, his last flight as a pilot in a military aircraft.

I can't imagine what his personal feelings must have been as he climbed out of the Chipmunk's cockpit at Hendon, completed the aircraft's Form 700 logbook with details of the flight and the aircraft's serviceability, and walked away. It was twenty years and two weeks after his first flight at Digby in an Avro Tutor with Sergeant Middleton; did he or Sergeant Middleton ever imagine where that flight would lead?

Cedric had flown a total of 2687 hours of which 1678 were as first pilot of single-engine aircraft and 698 as first pilot of multi-engine aircraft. He flew 53 distinct aircraft types – not including different marks of the same type – and he had a penchant and the ability for taking on unfamiliar aircraft without much, or any, formal instruction. He had shot down enemy aircraft, destroyed enemy shipping and probably killed. He had witnessed the death of subordinates flying under his leadership. He was not, by any means, one of the great RAF pilot heroes of WW2, but he had performed well beyond what might have been expected of an 'Average Pilot'.

Cedric was in Prague as British Air Attaché from 29 September 1955 until 22 April 1958. He and my mother lived in a large house in Prague and I travelled there to stay with them during each of the holidays from my English boarding school. In addition to a hectic social life, most of Cedric's duties would have centred on the gathering of information and the dissemination of misinformation. There are indications that he took avidly to these tasks. The following article from *Time* magazine of May 1957 gives a clue:

In recent weeks British and U.S. diplomats in Czechoslovakia have had the uncomfortable feeling that they were being followed. Two weeks ago the Foreign Ministry proudly produced results: British Air Attaché Group Captain Cedric Masterman and U.S. Air Attaché Colonel D.E. Teberg, they said, had been 'apprehended' in a 'clearly demarcated forbidden military zone'.

In separate answering notes, the U.S. and British ambassadors told what really happened. One sunny afternoon Group Captain Master-

man and Colonel Teberg, out for a picnic in the countryside, were driving along the main highway north of Prague in Masterman's car. At a crossroads near Milovice they were stopped by a military policeman and directed to turn off down a side road that bordered on an airfield. About 500 yds down the road, Masterman found his progress blocked by an army truck planted in the middle of the road. He stopped. Before he could turn around, another truck drove up close behind him, making any move impossible. Six soldiers with submachine guns appeared and surrounded the car. With car and officers pinned there, the Czechs briskly towed two twin-engined jets as close to the car as they could, then ran two tanks up close on the other side. Four photographers arrived. The blocking trucks were moved back, the gun-carrying guards retreated out of lens range, and the photographers then took photographs of the car against this 'most studiously arranged background'.

Some of the ground tours that he had had, the unexplained gaps in his flying and some of his circle of friends that I remember, all point to him having been engaged in intelligence activities at other times in his RAF career. But that is a side to his life that is long past and best left unexplored now.

His last formal day of service was 22 May 1958, but he was probably learning his new job of foreign exchange broker in the City of London a few weeks before then. In 1976 at the age sixty-two he retired as chairman of his company to live comfortably in a flat in Putney, London and a bungalow in Sleaford.

The phone rang at 2.30 a.m. on the morning of 5 May 2000. It was a staff member of Glenside Manor calling to say that Cedric had been taken ill and was on his way in an ambulance to Salisbury Hospital. Ruth and I got dressed and set off for the hospital which was only a few minutes away. We found Cedric unconscious in a recovery room, being attended by a doctor and nurse. We were told that Cedric had had a stroke, had been fitted with an intravenous line and bladder catheter, appeared comfortable, and there was nothing else to be done except wait to see what might happen over the next few hours. We took it in turns to stay with him for the remainder of that night and all of the following day.

I tried talking to him but he was completely unresponsive, breathing very heavily. I knew, of course, that he was dying. Alone together, my thoughts raced through my life's experiences with him: his war anecdotes related in the snugness of the cosy pubs he had loved, my difficult times with him while a teenager, the years while I was building my career during which we hardly met, and the experience of being responsible for him in his final years. For the first time in my life I knew that I loved him, and bitterly reflected that I should have realised that earlier in my life.

Always a handsome man, Cedric's hands were particularly attractive. They lay on top of the hospital sheet at rest: well manicured and still looking strong despite the paper thinness of the skin, an intravenous line running into the back of his right one. I thought of all those hands had done for him during his flying days.

I imagined him at the controls of a heavily laden Beaufighter lining up for take-off on Luqa runway in Malta, with Gordon Burnside to his rear as his navigator. He would have been grasping the ring handle at the top of the control column in one hand, advancing the throttles of the two Bristol Hercules engines with the other; countering the initial swing of the aircraft with his feet on the rudder pedals as the propellers began to bite and their 3000 horsepower-induced wash pressed against the tail fin.

Then, as the tail rose and induced a gyroscopic yaw from the changing axis of the propellers, he would adjust pedal pressure until the aircraft became aerodynamically stabilised by its rising speed. He would have been ever mindful, however, of the possible failure of an engine during the take-off run which might produce a sudden yaw and roll of the aircraft; only an immediate and correct response from him would then have prevented a premature and catastrophic end to the sortie.

I imagined the aircraft later, flying just twenty feet above the surface of the Mediterranean Sea, throttles wide open, directly into defensive fire from some Italian ship; and Cedric arming the aircraft's weapons, and triggering the guns or rockets from a switch on the control column.

As I sat by his side, I recalled him telling me how he prepared for his first flight in a strange aircraft. He would sit in the cockpit studying the Pilots Handbook and identify the purpose and location of every instrument, switch and control. He would call out the function for each and at the same time locate it with one of his hands. He would then continue this practice with his eyes closed until everything could be immediately touched without skinning his knuckles. His story was in those innocuous-looking, immobile hands.

In the afternoon a consultant neurologist spoke to me. He said that he could perform brain scans to determine the extent of damage caused by the stroke, but in his opinion the damage was already severe and Cedric was unlikely to recover consciousness. He added that even if Cedric did awaken he would certainly have physical impairment, probably serious, in addition to his dementia – quality of life would be very poor and likely short. I knew where his remarks were leading, so when he suggested that I might want to consider no resuscitation if there were to be another event, I was ready to agree. I asked that Cedric be made as comfortable as possible during what I realised would be his last hours.

Ruth and I stayed with Cedric until about midnight that day and then went home for some rest. At seven the next morning I was telephoned by the hospital to be told that Cedric had just died. When I got to his bed I found him lying on his back, eyes closed, a slight smile on his lips, and a rose placed on his chest by one of the nurses. I said my good-byes.

I helped pen an obituary for him that appeared in the *Daily Telegraph*. He was buried next to my mother in the Sleaford cemetery, after a well-attended service in the local Anglican Church at which I gave a eulogy summarising his life.

I received several letters from people that had known him. Some were from his Sleaford friends, others from City of London business associates. Two letters came from elderly ladies who had known him when he had still been flying in the RAF – one of whom had been taught to fly by him in Singapore; they were full of intense admiration.

15

Tailpiece

With the passing of Cedric I had felt that at last I could train for a pilot's licence of my own without the – completely irrational – feeling that I was in some way trying to emulate him. I had flown enough times as an engineer on test flights during my service career to know that I had no natural ability as a pilot but, nevertheless, I started my flying training at Old Sarum airfield, near Salisbury, from where Cedric had flown in a Hawker Audax in 1936. After 15 hours of instruction I went solo on 6 August 2000.

Ruth and I had wanted to return to Canada for several years so as to be near our two daughters but had been prevented by our willing obligation to look after Cedric. Thus, after his death, I gradually prepared for the move. I left the company for which I was then happily working and started up my own business consultancy with clients in both the UK and Canada.

Ruth and I arrived in Vancouver in November 2000. Sadly, we soon drifted apart, separated and then divorced four years later.

I finished training for my Private Pilot's Licence in 2001 at Boundary Bay Airport, 15 miles South of Vancouver.

One day in 2003 I took a Cessna 172 by myself on a round trip through the mountains north of Vancouver. I had recently taken a mountain flying course and felt confident in my abilities to navigate through mountain passes, and I had flown this particular route, Boundary Bay – Burrard Inlet – Howe Sound – Squamish – Indian Arm – Boundary Bay, twice before. I had filed a flight plan and took off in good weather which was forecast to continue all day. I approached Squamish on a northerly track on the east side of Howe Sound and then turned east into a mountain pass which would take me over the waters of Indian Arm. I had been flying at 3000 ft and so initiated a climb to 4500 ft which would take me clear of the top of the pass by 500 ft.

The valley stretched for about five miles in front of me, climbing and narrowing to the top of the pass which was snow covered, as were the mountain tops on either side of me. Clouds started to appear on my limited horizons and the sun was behind me provoking glare from the snow crystals. The aircraft continued to climb steadily; I was not seeking a maximum rate of climb because I did not want to have my view of the end of the valley obscured by raising the nose of the aircraft too much. The cloud backdrop to the pass thickened and I suddenly realised that the juxtaposition of cloud, snow and sunshine had melded my view into a white mass; I could no longer make out the top of the pass and my forward horizon had disappeared. I knew that I had to turn back immediately towards Squamish.

By now the valley was quite narrow and I judged it as probably too restricted for a normal Rate One 180-degree turn. I would have to perform a mountain turn, a sort of wingover that I had been taught during my mountain flying course. I quickly raised the aircraft's nose, watched the airspeed drop below 85 knots, selected 30 degrees of flap, and banked hard to the left. The aircraft turned and climbed sharply. There was something else I had to do: my right hand hovered by the electric flap selector lever; I felt a another, stronger hand embrace mine and guide it to the throttle which I advanced to full power. The aircraft reversed its track safely as I breathed 'Thank you, Cedric', and I returned to Boundary Bay without further incident.

This Large Print Book, for people
who cannot read normal print,
is published under the auspices of

THE ULVERSCROFT FOUNDATION